W9-CBH-761

MY *Greatest* SHOT

THE TOP PLAYERS
SHARE THEIR DEFINING
GOLF MOMENTS

MY
Greatest
SHOT

RON CHERNEY AND MICHAEL ARKUSH

HarperResource
An Imprint of HarperCollinsPublishers

HarperCollins books may be purchased for educational, business, or sales promotional use. For information please write: Special Markets Department, HarperCollins Publishers Inc., 10 East 53rd Street, New York, NY 10022.

Player photographs © AP Worldwide
El Caballero Country Club photographs © Doug Meadows and Gene Cofsky

FIRST EDITION

Printed on acid-free paper

Book design by William Ruoto

Library of Congress Cataloging-in-Publication Data

My greatest shot : the top players share their defining golf moments / [compiled by] Ron Cherney and Michael Arkush.— 1st ed.
      p. cm.
    ISBN 0-06-056278-1
    1. Golfers—United States—Biography. I. Cherney, Ron. II. Arkush, Michael.

GV964.A1M9 2004
796.352'092'2—dc22
[B]   2003067763

05 06 07 08 ❖/QW 10 9 8 7 6

For Lisa,
who never misses a fairway or
green and makes every putt.
—Ron Cherney

To Pauletta,
whose greatness comes
in many ways.
—Michael Arkush

— Contents —

MY
Greatest
SHOT

— *Introduction* —

I have followed the greats—Sam, Byron, Ben, Arnold, Gary, Tom, Mickey, and, of course, Jack—for as long as I can remember. They are my heroes, every one of them, able to perform the impossible.

I have listened to the experts analyze every swing, drive, and putt, defining for us the greatest shots in the history of the game. I have, however, always wondered what the players themselves think.

In the summer of 1999, I decided to find out. I mailed letters to more than 200 players, asking for the best shot they ever hit, and, if possible, the best shot they ever witnessed. I was under no illusions. I was merely another anonymous fan asking them for something.

To my amazement, the responses poured in, starting with, appropriately enough, Tom Watson, who described one of the most memorable shots of all time, the chip-in on the 17th hole at Pebble Beach in the 1982 U.S. Open. It soon became clear that the players were giving the matter serious thought. The responses came in many forms—handwritten notes, typed letters, faxes, e-mails, and, in one case, a Post-it.

Some wrote page after page, filled with tremendous emotion. These letters, I realized, were helping the players recapture a moment that meant so much to them. It was particularly thrilling to hear from the older ones, whose skills may have diminished, yet whose memories have not.

On several occasions, I was lucky enough to speak to them. Betty Jameson, who won the 1947 U.S. Women's Open, shared stories of playing with Babe Zaharias and receiving tips from Ben Hogan. The late Johnny Bulla told of hitchhiking to Georgia to watch the construction of Augusta National, sleeping in parked cars to save money. Jack Fleck, who shocked the golf universe by beating Ben Hogan at the 1955 U.S. Open, recalled his days as head professional at El Caballero Country Club, the club where I belong. Their voices were as powerful as their written words. As a golf fan, I was in awe.

The collection grew to an overstuffed binder that I rarely let out of my sight. I couldn't wait to share the latest letter with my friends. Soon, another idea hit me: Why not turn these letters into a book?

Fortunately, a big break came when I was playing golf at the majestic Ojai Valley Inn & Spa with my lovable, sandbagging brother-in-law, Brad Shames. We caught up to a twosome in front of us. One of the players happened to be Michael Arkush, a former associate editor of *Golf World* and author of five books. Michael loved the idea from the start. He suggested that the letters be accompanied by brief biographical sketches of each player, along with fresh quotes. In several cases, we included highlights of the player's achievements.

Michael, it seems, knows every golfer going back to Old Tom Morris. Through Michael's perseverance and determination, we made it our mission to contact every top player. We went to numerous events, handing out letters on the driving range and putting green.

We heard from Notah Begay about the shot he hit as a boy, a shot that only he saw. We heard from Donna Caponi about the time she ignored Byron Nelson's commentary—and won the U.S. Women's Open. We heard from David Feherty, whose Road Hole story was printed in his January 2003 *Golf Magazine* column. We heard from Jack Nicklaus, Tiger Woods, and Arnold Palmer. Tim Finchem and Ty Votaw wrote about the best shots they had ever seen. They are more than just commissioners. They are fans.

In order to preserve the true spirit of the project, the letters were not altered, for the most part. As a result, the responses include typos, misspelled words, incomplete sentences, and inaccurate recollections. Sam Snead's shot, for instance, did not win the 1950 Los Angeles Open but earned him a playoff with Ben Hogan. The shot on the 18th hole at Riviera was, nonetheless, outstanding.

There are many types of great shots, from Brad Faxon's putt to Joey Sindelar's ace, from Arnold Palmer's three-wood to Curtis Strange's blast from the bunker. The venues varied, from the local muni to Augusta National. Several players, not surprisingly, picked a shot from the PGA Tour's Q-School, the most grueling test in professional golf.

But there was always one element in common; a deep, unconditional love for the game, and a realization that, for one moment at least, these tremendous players had achieved the perfection they chased for years.

Michael and I have added our own greatest shots, and have left space at the back of the book for you to do the same.

For all of us, our next shot could be our greatest.

Ron Cherney
January 2004

Timothy W. Finchem
Commissioner

June 14, 2002

Dear Dr. Cherney:

Congratulations on your novel idea of collecting individual letters detailing the finest shots of all-time.

In my position, I have been privileged to see a number of memorable shots at PGA TOUR events from some of the greatest players in the game. At THE PLAYERS Championship alone, for example, I've seen Fred Couples' brilliant eagle on #16, Tiger Woods' long birdie putt on #17 and Jerry Pate's 5-iron to the 18th hole. Long before my time there were historic shots from Gene Sarazen, Sam Snead, Ben Hogan and too many others to list.

Since the question, however, is the single greatest shot I have ever witnessed, I would select the 1-iron that Jack Nicklaus hit to the 17th green at the 1972 U.S. Open at Pebble Beach.

I was a law student at the University of Virginia at that time and had no idea that I would one day end up having the privilege of working with so many of these great players and being witness to many of the game's greatest moments.

I wish you much success with your venture and hope that you are able to generate a sizable donation to your selected charitites.

Sincerely,

Timothy W. Finchem

Ladies   Professional   Golf   Association

Ty M. Votaw
Commissioner

June 28, 2002

Dear Ron:

I've been with the LPGA for more than 11 years now—and a fan much longer than that—and I have seen some incredible golf by legends of the game and rising stars. Choosing just one shot as my favorite proved to be a tough task, and, in the end, I am forced to submit to you *two* shots that stand out in my memory, two shots that are inexorably linked, one making the other even more incredible.

At the 1998 Solheim Cup at Muirfield Village Golf Club, I was watching the Saturday afternoon four-ball match between Juli Inkster/Meg Mallon and Liselotte Neumann/Charlotta Sorenstam. It was a battle all day, and the U.S. pair got to the 17th hole with a 1 up lead. Liselotte hit what I think has to be one of the world's best greenside bunker shots to about 2 inches, and it looked as if the Europeans would tie the match and force it to go to the 18th hole. Judy Rankin, who has seen dozens of PGA Tour players in that same bunker over the years at the PGA Tour's Memorial tournament during her work as an on-course commentator for ABC Sports, later said that it was one of the greatest bunker shots she had ever seen.

Then, just seconds later, Juli drained a 45-footer right on top of Liselotte's shot to win the hole and the match. The atmosphere was truly electrifying as the hometown crowd went wild. As an aside, if I was asked about the most memorable dance move—it would be Juli's whirling, twirling celebration after the putt dropped in. She should not get many style points, but her uncontainable excitement was contagious.

That series of events will forever give me goose bumps. And it has nothing to do with the fact that the LPGA came out on top—regardless of Tour affiliation or nationality, I witnessed one of the most memorable and exciting moments in the history of women's golf.

Sincerely,

Ty M. Votas

Ty M. Votaw

TMV:3067/mts

AmyAlcott
GOLF OUTINGS ● COURSE DESIGN ● PRODUCT SPOKESPERSON

APR.
22,
2003

Dear Ron,

Thank you for your letter of interest in my greatest golf shot ever hit. There have been several, but, the one that sticks out is the 25 foot putt I made to win my very first tournament, Feb 22, 1975 at Pasadena Golf Club, St. Petersburg, Florida. I didn't know I was tied for the lead going into the last hole, a par 5, I was shot in two.. hit a poor chip to about 25 feet. I didn't look at the leaderboard, but I could feel a sense of importance. I lined the putt up & it went in for a birdie & a one-stroke victory. It was a most amazing moment that I will remember always. It was only my 3RD pro tournament.

My best golfing wishes,

Amy Alcott

Amy Alcott

In 1975, two years after winning the U.S. Junior Girls' title, Amy Alcott made the jump to the big leagues. She captured the two most prestigious events on the LPGA Tour—the U.S. Open (1980) and the Nabisco Dinah Shore (1983, 1988, 1991). Alcott, who has 29 victories, finished in the Top 10 on the money list every season from 1978 through 1986. In 1999, Alcott, 48, was inducted into the LPGA Tour Hall of Fame.

OPEN FIRE: "It was a pretty amazing feeling, at 24 years old, which was awfully young, to win the Open. The temperature in Nashville was well over 100 degrees, one of the hottest summers in U.S. history. To succeed in heat like that was a real personal triumph. I played some of the greatest golf of my career. Because it was so hot, it made it easier for me to go into the zone that it takes to win. I was thinking of just surviving, of staying upright. I wore lots of ice around my neck and drank a lot of water. I was also in very good condition, which helped me. I was even out running the week before in heat."

JUMPING IN THE LAKE WITH DINAH: "It was a spontaneous thing. I figured, let's go have some fun. It was warm, so it was the thing to do. My caddie and I did it together first [in 1988, at Mission Hills Country Club in Rancho Mirage, California]. A few years later, we pulled Dinah in. She wanted to go in. She was an amazing person, so passionate about women's golf. She realized even more than women do today that we are in the entertainment business. If more players could understand that, we'd be even further along than we are now. It took a woman like that to be at the forefront of a major women's tournament."

I AM WOMAN, HEAR ME ROAR: "Women have to have more of a sense of entitlement. Competing for women is still a relatively new thing because women are more nurturing. I was watching the Grammy Awards recently. If you see a woman get an award, she's almost apologetic where a man wouldn't be. The biggest key for a woman is to feel like she deserves to be there, just as much as anyone else. She should just go ahead and enjoy herself."

PETER ALLISS - GOLF LIMITED

It was at the 18th hole at Royal Birkdale, the Ryder Cup of 1965.   Alliss and O'Connor versus Marr and Palmer, the match situation being 1 up.   I put my second shot with a 4-wood about 10ft from the hole and they could not do better than a 5, so we had won, having lost to them 6 and 4 in the morning's play.   It was a long way for a 4-wood but I remembered a tip from John Jacobs.   I toed the club in a little bit, aimed down the right-hand side, the wind was coming a little from the right, boom, I hit it right out of the button.   It was a wonderful shot, I can see it now, and it is only about the 6th shot I ever remember playing!

Peter Alliss

Peter Alliss

England's Peter Alliss, 73, a longtime golf commentator for ABC, was a very accomplished player in Europe for much of the 1950s and 1960s, seizing three British PGA Championships and participating in eight Ryder Cups. Alliss, with 23 triumphs on his resume, made his broadcasting debut with the BBC at the 1961 British Open. Alliss, who has written 20 books, is recognized for his wit and humor.

TELLING IT LIKE IT IS: "When I was young, I was fortunate enough to get with some people who could think on their feet. I had that sort of brain that accumulated little sayings and remarks. I'm very observant. I can go into a room and look at it for five seconds and see the pictures, a paper on the floor, two cigarettes in an ashtray, that the time is twenty past four. I see things immediately."

HOME SWEET HOME: "I came to the United States and played eight weeks on the tour in 1954. I covered my expenses. In those days, if you finished out of the top dozen, you were lucky to make $30, that sort of thing. I was married, had a child, and had to make a living. The desire to come play in the United States was very different back then. My mother and father and brother were still alive. I wasn't impoverished. It wasn't like the Irish potato famine. We weren't going to the Promised Land. The great myth is if you don't make it in the United States, you're a failure. I think that's wrong."

LESS LOVE FOR THE LINKS: "I was brought up on heather and pine trees and silver birch trees and inland golf courses and little loops of three and four holes, where you go out in the evening and potter about, whereas the great links courses, in most cases, go straight out and straight back. They're magical to look at on a lovely day with good companions and four decent caddies, but to go out in wind and rain, it's not fun. What would be the fun of being a member at Augusta if they played under tournament conditions all the time?"

RICH BEEM

There were some great shots I hit at the International and the PGA in 2002 but there was one shot years earlier that I think helped me play as well as I did down the stretch in those two wins.

It wasn't really the best shot I've ever hit but under the circumstances....

Going into the last hole at Kingsmill back in 2001 we were tied for seventh. We knew we needed to make about $100,000 to keep my card and I somehow figured out how to hit a 3-wood right down the middle. That left us with about 190 to the pin on the top-right tier where they always put it on Sunday.

I hit a 6-iron that never left the flagstick, was just all over it. I was so nervous, shaking so bad, and I just striped it right at it. It hit in the middle of the hill and kicked up but then it came back down, unfortunately. But I two-putted and made 101 grand to keep my card. That was kind of a big moment because I had been struggling for a while.

That 6-iron gave me the confidence to know that if I ever came down to a really pressure-packed situation I could do it again. That was kind of it. Knowing my card was on the line. Hitting those may be easier when you're winning a tournament because you're already playing well. But if you haven't been playing well and you need to come up with something big...that was probably one of the biggest shots I ever hit.

Now there were some great shots at the PGA at Hazeltine. On 11 in the final round, we had 248 front, I think 272 to the hole. I hit what I like to call my 7-wood. It was actually an 18-degree Taylor Made fairway wood. We were on a little upslope and the wind was a little left to right and helping and it was just a perfect shot. I absolutely clobbered it, which was nice, but it was just one of those shots that if you hit it perfect, it's going to go the perfect distance.

On 16 that day we had a putt of about 35 feet or so. What kind of made it difficult was that it was kind of going up the hill but once it got up there it kind of turned away from me and turned left. We just picked a spot about a foot out, right on top of the hill. If we could hit that spot it was going to be pretty good. I don't even remember hitting the putt to be honest with you. I just remember looking up. Once it got to the top of the hill, I knew it was going to be close. Once it started turning left I knew it had the right speed and it went right into the heart at perfect speed. I had been putting well all week, but that was clearly the biggest putt of the week by far. It was just a great putt at a very fortunate time. I was so pumped up I was actually lucky. When I threw the ball in the water after the putt I could have thrown my arm out and hobbled in.

Those were both big shots but they really went back to that 6-iron on the 18th hole at Kingsmill.

Rich Beem

Rich Beem, 33, sold car stereos and cellular phones in the mid-1990s, but it wasn't until the 2002 PGA Championship at Hazeltine Golf Club that he turned up the volume, defeating Tiger Woods down the stretch to snare his first major. Beem, who prevailed two weeks before in Colorado, became golf's newest sensation, finishing seventh on the money list with almost $3 million. In 2003, he picked up another major prize, a baby boy.

FATHERHOOD: "People gave me all this advice, but you mostly take that advice and throw it out the window. Your kid is going to be your kid, and you've got to kind of deal with it the way you're going to deal with it. It's been fantastic. All of a sudden, everything revolves around him and that is a good thing. I'm enjoying the hell out of it. Everything you do has a purpose, because he is the purpose."

LIFE AFTER THE PGA: "I'm enjoying all the perks, but it's only one tournament. Of course, I'd like to win more majors. It changes your vision a little, but you can't say, 'Now that I've won this, I'm a great player. I should do this every week.' My game is not like that. Just because I won something big like that doesn't mean that you're going to do that every single week. Sometimes, it gets strange. When I'm walking down the fairway and I'm a couple strokes over par, and someone is screaming, 'Wow, you're the Beemer, you're the man, way to go,' it's like, 'Have you seen my scorecard lately?'"

ONE DAY AT A TIME: "It's great to win tournaments, but as soon as you think you've got this thing figured out, you're going to get knocked right on your ass again, and you better be prepared for that. I try to be as humble as I can. I just went out and played golf and made it up as I went along. Greg Norman had the seven-year plan. I got no plan. I'm planning on waking up tomorrow, having a good day, and having a beer after my round, and that's about it. I don't overanalyze. As soon as I do, I get all screwed up."

NOTAH R. BEGAY III

Ironically, the greatest shot of my life can't be found on any PGA Tour highlight reel or in any golf magazines. That's because I'm the only one that was there when it happened. I was eleven years old and had decided to try and squeeze nine holes in before dark but couldn't find a playing partner. It was a perfect summer evening so I proceeded to go alone for a casual round before dinner. The fifth hole at my home course (Ladera Municipal) is a 160-yard par three, and at that time in my life was anywhere between a five iron and seven iron. On that day, there was a slight breeze into my face and the club of choice was a five iron to a pin located just past the middle of the green. This particular hole is not all that difficult, it doesn't have any bunkers or hazards and the green is generous in size. So one would wonder how such a hole could leave such a lasting impression in my mind and on my career.

The green was set against the backdrop of a beautiful New Mexico sunset which made it difficult to see the ball in flight. So immediately after contact I was unable to find the ball between the magnificent rays of sunlight and had no idea as to the outcome. All I had to rely on was the feel of the shot and that it seemed to take off on line but I would have to wait and see. I came upon the green and the ball was nowhere in sight. So I searched the green for a few minutes and turned up nothing. Of course, my very last inclination was to look in the hole which I did sometime later and therein rested my destiny. Being overrun with energy and excitement I quickly jumped up to see if anyone had somehow witnessed my untimely achievement but found nobody. In the long run that didn't really matter because that one shot is when the game of golf truly captured me for life. In that one moment, I realized its perfection, a perfection and purity which I strive for to this day.

Summer of '83

Notah Begay III

Notah Begay III, the most successful Native American to ever play golf at the highest level, has never abandoned his roots, giving clinics on reservations throughout the Southwest. Begay, 31, attended Stanford in the 1990s with Tiger Woods and Casey Martin, and was a member of the school's 1994 NCAA Championship squad. For years, Begay putted left- and right-handed, depending on the break.

PUTT IT THIS WAY: "I stopped halfway through last year. I know there is a lot of upside to putting both ways, but my consistency on a week-to-week basis wasn't that great. I just figured I'd try to simplify it, so I went right-handed. The game is hard enough without trying to make it more difficult. I've put together some consistent putting weeks, so I know there's some potential to really become a good putter."

INDIAN COUNTRY: "Being the only Native American on the tour provides a lot of responsibility. I don't take that as a burden. I look to it as an opportunity to go out there and make a difference and act as a role model. I relish the fact that I come from a diverse background. It makes me extremely happy to know that I may have a positive impact on somebody. Golf is growing in Indian Country, and I would like to think I have a little bit to do with that. It's great to see junior players have a grasp of the mechanics. They understand that it does take a lot of hard work, and that the principles the game is built upon are principles that I would choose to implement with any child: discipline, respect, and sportsmanship. Those are things we can all use in our lives."

PRETTY GOOD COMPANY: "Playing golf at Stanford was a fairly surreal experience. Looking at what Tiger Woods has done and what I've done on tour and the achievements of Casey Martin and what he was fighting for, to have that type of talent at one school on one team at one time, I look back, and say, 'Did it really happen?' "

October 10, 2000

Dear Dr. Cherney:

In answer to your letter August 22, I find it difficult to think of a personal "greatest" shot. On a given day at a given place and under given circumstances, canning a 10-foot putt might rank as a "greatest" shot. On other days under other circumstances, threading through some trees and having the ball stop three feet from the cup may be a "greatest" shot.

Anyone who tees it up in earnest hits great and not-so-great shots, their memorability only of the moment in that there's always tomorrow when an even greater shot may be hit. I hit a lot of great shots as well as a lot of shots I wish I could have hit over again. Even today, at age 82, when I chip or pitch within a foot of the cup, I deem it a "great" shot.

So no, Dr. Cherney, an evaluation of my "great" shots would have to come from someone else, for I find it impossible to select one above others I may have hit.

Now as to great shots I've seen (and this only on television), I think anyone who saw it would be hard pressed to surpass Tiger Woods' shot out of the bunker on the 18th hole of the final round of this year's Canadian Open. It was a true dazzler, and anyone who knows a 7-iron from a hockey puck would have to be as impressed by it as I was and still am.

Good luck with your project, and thanks for thinking of me.

Cordially,

Patty Berg

Patty J Berg

Patty Berg

Patty Berg captured her first professional tournament in 1941, and her last in 1962, the Muskogee Civitan Open. Overall, she won 60 events, becoming, in 1950, one of the 13 founding members of the LPGA Tour. Among her accomplishments were 15 major championships—more than any woman in the history of the game. Berg, 86, served as a lieutenant in the U.S. Marine Corps during World War II.

THE FEW, THE PROUD: "I'm very proud to have been a U.S. Marine. During my service with the Corps, I learned a lot about myself, and—more importantly—a lot about other people. Up to that point, I had led a somewhat insulated life—golf and more golf—but service in the Corps exposed me to people from all walks of life, and I came to appreciate even further the broad range of human actions, emotions, and opinions. I felt at the time and still do that my assigned recruiting duties made a significant contribution to our country's overall war effort."

NO SISSIES: "[In the Minnesota neighborhood where I grew up], we played tackle, none of that sissy 'touch football' stuff for us. I was the team's quarterback, supposedly because I was the only one who could remember the signals for our plays. There were, essentially, two: Run for daylight, and scatter and try to catch what's thrown in your direction. Bud Wilkinson, later the famed football coach at the University of Oklahoma, was the team's captain and spark plug. Eventually, it was Bud who told me I was off the team because I was too small and too slow. I was crushed, but my mother was much relieved. Not only were my teeth still intact, but I no longer would be coming home with scraped knees and elbows and torn skirts."

START SOMEWHERE: "My father played golf. One day, I took a club out of his bag, went into our backyard, and proceeded to slash great gobs of turf out of our lawn, hacking blooms from several of his prize roses. Following an appropriate parental lecture about responsibility, he asked me if I really wanted to play golf, and when I said yes, he made arrangements for me to take lessons at his club."

Tommy Bolt

In reply to your letter, the 6 iron shot I hit on the 18 hole in the 1956 Colonial Invitation in Ft. Worth, Texas, was one of the greatest shots I ever hit. Leading the Tournament the first three rounds, I was in the last group off. Mike Sonchak was two groups in front. He was in the Clubhouse with a great round of 65. I was on the 16th hole when I heard about it. I needed three birdies to tie. I parred the 16th, birdied the 17th. Now I needed a two on Par 4 18th. I drove in the Fairway on the right side perfect position with a 6 iron left to the hole to try for the two I needed for a tie. I put the best swing possible on the 6 iron, carried two feet short, clipped the hole and stopped six inches past. I didn't win but gave it a good shot.

Thanks,
TOMMY BOLT

Tommy Bolt

Tommy Bolt

Tommy Bolt was known as "Thunder Bolt" or "Terrible Tommy" for his habit of throwing clubs. But Bolt possessed something else besides a temper. He possessed talent, with 15 official victories, highlighted by the 1958 United States Open at Southern Hills in Oklahoma, when he held off the youngster, Gary Player, by four strokes. In 1971, at 55, he finished third in the PGA Championship.

AGE IS ONLY A NUMBER: "I can beat players that are 60 years old—I know that. I'm 87. Find me some 87-year-old men to play me, can you? I shoot from 75 to 80. When I get to 80, I'm coming in. I'm a little shorter than I was because I'm not as flexible, but I hit some drives today that went 230, maybe 240 yards. I play golf every time that it doesn't rain. I'm always working on it, always trying to improve. That's just the way golf is. You never conquer golf."

NOT SO TERRIBLE TOMMY: "Bob Hope once said that any publicity is good publicity. He must have known something. Yes, I showed a little temper out there, but not as bad as the press ballooned it. They overdid it. I never killed anybody. I wasn't a John Dillinger, but they made it sound like that. How many clubs has Tiger Woods thrown? Nobody says a word about how many clubs he throws."

WE HAD MORE FUN: "Today's tour players are spoiled rotten. There is so much money that it's unbelievable, and they don't appreciate it at all. They don't have the fun that we had out there. When you get big money involved, it's very serious business. They're stronger and the equipment is better, and the golf courses are better manicured. But we had it the best. We knew everybody when we came to a city. Now, when the kids leave the golf course, their manager takes them right back to their room."

JOHNNY BULLA

Dear Ron,

       In response to your request about the greatest shots I have ever seen or hit, I want to say that I have seen a lot of great shots and hit a lot I would have liked to take over. I'd have to say the best shot I ever hit was during the 1961 Southern California Open held at Indian Wells. I had just won the Long Beach Match Play Championship at Rec Park and was leading after the first day. In the 2nd round I was on the 12th hole when Jerry Barber was on the 11th fairway and yelled over to me, "Johnny, you can win a match play tournament but you can't win a medal one". I made a 2 on the par 3 12th, then knocked a three wood in the hole on the par 5 13th for a double eagle, then made a 2 on the par 3 14th. Three straight 2's!!! I've been lucky to have 6 holes in one but really lucky to have had 8 double eagles.

       There are a couple of shots that I can think of that I saw that were great. Ben Hogan's 2 iron at the 18th hole at Merion was special. I also remember playing with Bobby Jones at Eastlake. He had hit into a bunker on the par 3 10th that was pretty steep faced. Now he never had a sand wedge and I could not figure out how he was going to get a 9 iron out. He always hooded his 9 iron and did so this time but on his downswing, he opened up the blade to have the ball come out nice and soft for a gimmee. He had the best hands.

       A funny shot I remember was when I was playing Jim Turnesa in the PGA at Richmond, Virginia in the first round. On the 17th hole, I was one up with a 3 foot putt for birdie. Turnesa laid a stymie on me and was lying 4. I decided to hit his ball hard and ended up knocking his into the hole! I missed the 1 ½ footer and lost the hole and then 3 putted 18 to lose the match

       On a side note, I'm proud of the fact that I was the first PGA pro to play with an African American in 1944, with a young man named Sears. He was a caddy from New Orleans who could really play. Unfortunately, he was killed the next year in the war.

       I hope this helps and I look forward to seeing your book soon.

Regards,

Johnny Bulla

Johnny Bulla

In the record books, Johnny Bulla is credited with only one official tour victory, the 1941 Los Angeles Open. But Bulla, a regular on the tour in the 1930s, '40s, and '50s, was a winner in many other ways. Like many in his era, he started as a caddie, learning about the game and about life. During World War II, he worked as a commercial pilot. Bulla died in December 2003 at the age of 89.

IF THEY BUILD IT, HE WILL GO: "I hitchhiked down there [to Augusta National] in 1932, 300 miles from my home, to see them build it. The talk was that it was going to be super, and I wanted to see it. This was during the Depression, and I didn't have any money. I saved up just enough that I could eat on, but I'd sleep in a car at night. There were open cars, and when the sun went down, I'd sneak into the back seat and sleep there until the daylight. I was 18 years old. I stayed down there for a couple of weeks."

BREAKING OTHER GROUND: "I told George S. May to hold a tournament with blacks and I would be glad to play. He paired me with Calvin Searles, who was moving from the European theater in World War II to the Pacific. They gave him two weeks off before he had to go over there. We played as a twosome for 72 holes. A human being is a human being. I grew up in North Carolina, but for some reason I never bought into that racial prejudice stuff. Next to Tiger, I think Searles was the best black player I have ever seen. He finished seventh in our tournament with very little practice."

THE BABE: "During the qualifier for the L.A. Open, I played with Babe Zaharias. She was a great pal, but she could be a little cocky. On the first tee, she told me that she outdrives most of the men she plays with. After the fourth hole, when I had hit each of my drives about 40 yards past her, I said to her, 'Babe, you must be hitting it off the heel today.' She said, 'Shut up.' We got along great."

WILLIAM C. CAMPBELL

June 11, 2002

Dear Dr. Cherney:

 I am pleased to respond to the compliment of your request for a letter about my best golf shot and the best one I have ever seen by others.

 As for the latter, I have no doubt that the #1 prize belongs to one by the late George Richard Nicholas Huntington Nash, then #6 man at the '47 Princeton golf team that could only continue its unbeaten match record of '46 and '47 seasons if his 5 iron shot went into the hole on the par 3 #9 of Navy's North Savern Course– the last hole of the match, as we had started on #10. Princeton had to win that hole, for the only point at risk in the better-ball match; a Navy player was up close for a sure birdie 2 and Nash's partner was in the water, so the only hope for our team's victory over Navy and to maintain our own defeated record was the hole-in-one that happened! Everyone was so stunned that, for some seconds after this feat, no one made a sound; and then what they had seen sank in; you can guess the rest – bedlam for us, despair for Navy. Incidentally, Nash's feat was written up in Ripley's Believe It Or Not.

 As for my own best shot, it really wasn't much of a shot because I was putting off the road of the 17th hole of the Old Course in the second day's singles match of the 1975 Walker Cup at St. Andrews. This was my 8th Walker Cup singles over a span of 24 years, and at age 52 I didn't want to score my first such loss, especially since on the day before I had let a win turn into a halved match. Of course the road is always problematic, as my only shot was to bang the ball into the bank with the hope that it would get on the green and leave a makeable putt. Actually, I was left with only a tiddler to close out the match 2-1 and thus preserve my undefeated status. It may not have seemed such a great shot to others who saw it, but I was much relieved by the happy turn of events.

 Thank you for asking, and congratulations on what appears to be your wholehearted contribution to the lore of the game which we all love. I hope to meet you some day. Meanwhile best wishes.

 Sincerely,

 Bill Campbell

William Campbell

The numbers on longtime amateur William Campbell are extraordinary. He has participated in 37 U.S. Amateurs, 18 Masters, 15 U.S. Opens, and was a member of eight Walker Cup teams. He captured the U.S. Amateur in 1964 at Canterbury Golf Club in Cleveland and never lost a Walker Cup singles match. Campbell, 80, won the U.S. Senior Amateur in 1979 and 1980, and served as president of the USGA in 1982 and 1983.

SANTA DELIVERS: "In my eight Walker Cups, five of them were in Great Britain, including three in St. Andrews. If the Walker Cup means a lot to you and you are ever going to write a letter to Santa Claus, you want the competition to be overseas and especially at St. Andrews. I wasn't good enough in my salad days to win by very big margins, and I never did play as well in the alternate shot format as I did in the singles."

OVER THERE: "I went from the ROTC in Princeton to the ASTP—the Army Specialized Training Program. I served 19 months as an enlisted man, and then went to artillery school. I came out as a second lieutenant and was assigned to the training battery in Ft. Bragg. I was invited to join the 100th Infantry Division, and served in France and Germany with the division artillery. The 100th Division was very much in combat. I would not have wanted to stay in the military, but knowing the temper of the times and what World War II meant, it was the place to be and the thing to do."

OVER HERE: "I was a member of the West Virginia Legislature from 1948 to 1951, and ran for Congress in 1952, defeated by the incumbent in the Democratic primary. I later changed parties. I did not feel at home in the Democratic party, which was out of step in West Virginia, or I was. I ran for the State Senate in 1970 and 1974 as a Republican, again against an incumbent. I finally decided I wasn't a very good candidate and would rather help elect others."

Donna Caponi

For about two decades, Donna Caponi was one of the LPGA Tour's premier performers, a constant presence in the Top 20 on the money list. Caponi produced 24 victories, including four major championships. In 2001, she was voted into the LPGA Tour Hall of Fame through the Veteran's Category. Caponi, 59, works as a golf commentator/analyst for The Golf Channel and CBS.

SAVED BY SORENSTAM: "I was eating an apple at a tournament site in 2003 when one of the pieces went down the wrong pipe. Something lodged, and I had no air. Using the Heimlich maneuver, Charlotta Sorenstam whacked me and the apple fell out. As God is my witness, before she hit me, I was gone. I felt my eyes roll back because I had no air for what seemed like 20 or 30 seconds. I hugged her and thanked her. The next day, every time someone talked about it, I got more emotional."

DADDY'S GIRL: "My dad would go to the golf course on Saturday mornings. I was one of those kids who would wrap themselves around his leg as he went out the door because I wanted to go with him. I guess I was 4 or 5 years old. One morning he finally said, 'Okay, you can go with me. Why don't you pull my pull cart?' He cut off a club for me and put it in the bag. He would let me hit a shot, and the guys he would play with would go along with it. My father was everything to me. He was my father, my best friend, and my instructor."

TOUGH GRADER: "I was happy with my career. If I hadn't gotten into the Hall of Fame, I probably would have been very disappointed. Being the leading money-winner in any one year was something I really worked hard to get; I was always just a beat short. People think I'm nuts, but I never thought I was a great player; I thought I was a really good player. Great players are Mickey Wright, Kathy Whitworth, Nancy Lopez, Annika Sorenstam, Karrie Webb."

The Greatest Shot I Ever Hit

By Donna Caponi

Member, World Golf Hall of Fame

Dear Mike,

Five-foot putts are fairly commonplace. It's the circumstances surrounding this particular putt, and how it ultimately changed my life, which qualify this as the greatest shot I ever hit.

The scene of the crime: Scenic Hills Country Club, Pensacola, Florida in the 1969 U.S. Women's Open. And as it always does in the summer in Florida, the thunderstorms would arrive in the afternoon.

When I teed off Sunday morning, I was five shots out of the lead. After making a number of birdies, I arrived at the 18th tee with a great chance to win the tournament. On the tee box, we could hear the thunder in the background, which meant the storms were moving in. I hit my tee ball right down the middle of the dogleg par five. As I was getting set to hit my second, lightning flashed right over my head and, of course, play was called.

So I went into the clubhouse to the ladies locker room and stayed away from everybody just so I could keep my concentration in check. We were in there for one hour. Then we went back out.

Now keep in mind before the rain I thought I could reach the par five in two. But once we got back out the ground was very soft and so I changed my strategy, opting instead to lay up and just rely on my short game. I hit my second shot just short of the green, and then wedged to within five feet of the hole.

Unfortunately, I was above the hole, the cardinal sin in a major championship where the greens are extremely fast. As I'm lining up the putt, I've now realized that if I make the putt I will have won my first tournament after finishing second so many times. I read the putt from every possible angle.

So I get over the ball and I can hear the commentators whispering in the tower just behind the green. The commentators are no less than Jim McKay and Lord Byron Nelson himself. I hear Byron say in a low tone of voice, "If Donna makes this putt this could win her the U.S. Open."

He then says, "This putt will break right to left."

I hear him say this as I'm over the ball. At that point I step back because I had read it left to right. So I proceed to re-read the putt all over again, thinking that Byron Nelson couldn't be wrong. After all, he'd won 11 tournaments in a row, 18 in one year, major championships and was considered one of the greatest players in history. Talk about confusion.

Finally, with all due respect to Byron, I listened to the voice of my father. He always told me, "Go with your first instinct."

I step back up to the ball, hit the putt the way I read it—left to right—and lo and behold the putt goes in. I had won the U.S. Open.

In the media room I was asked why I stepped back from the putt. I told the press the story of how I heard Byron reading the putt opposite of what I had thought. Someone in the media quickly wondered if I'd seen the camera on the other side of the hole. They explained to me that Byron was reading the putt from the camera angle the viewers were seeing at home.

Normally when a man like Byron Nelson speaks you listen. Thank goodness on this occasion I went with my gut.

I've had lunch with Byron several times since, and he always asks, "Thank goodness you didn't listen to me or you wouldn't have won the U.S. Open."

THE GREATEST SHOT I HIT HAPPENED IN THE 1970 MASTERS PLAY OFF WITH GENE LITTLER. AFTER SCORING BIRDIE ON THE FIRST HOLE, I MADE A VERY BAD SWING ON DRIVE OFF THE SECOND TEE. DUCK HOOK HITTING PINE TREE TO LEFT OF THE FAIRWAY, BALL BOUNCED LEFT INTO WATER HAZARD FAR LEFT OF FAIRWAY, NO WATER IN HAZARD ONLY TALL GRASS WHICH HAD BEEN TRAMPLED DOWN BY THE MASSIVE GALERYES. BALL RESTED ON TOP OF GRASS WITH A BRANCH COVERING HALF THE BALL ABOUT TWO INCHES BEHIND THE BALL. ONLY SHOT WAS A NINE IRON FITTING THE CLUB OVER BRANCH UNDER THE BALL. THE STRIKING OF THE MUST BE PERFECT HAD TO CARRY OF TALL PINE TREES BACK TO FAIRWAY ABOUT 140 YARDS RESULTS PERFECT SHOT A PAR FIVE TWO SHOT LEAD AND ONTO WINNING 1970 MASTER CASPER 69 LITTLER 74 ANY SCORE MUCH HIGHER COULD HAVE RESULTED — MY GREATEST SHOT.

Billy Casper

Billy Casper, 72, a 5-time Vardon Trophy winner, will be forever remembered for rallying from a seven-stroke deficit against Arnold Palmer with nine holes to play in the final round of the 1966 U.S. Open at The Olympic Club in San Francisco. Casper prevailed in an 18-hole playoff the following day. One of the game's most underrated stars and brilliant putters, Casper won 51 tournaments, including the 1959 U.S. Open and the 1970 Masters.

AN OLYMPIC MOMENT: "When he went to the back nine, because he had such a large lead, Palmer had the goal of establishing a record. As he made a couple of bogeys and I made a birdie or two, he panicked. The little fat boy was right on his heels. It's the only time I ever saw him panic. He kept pulling the ball off the tee and not hitting it a great distance. He wasn't free and smooth, as he had been in the early part of the round. Of course, it encouraged me tremendously. When I birdied the 15th hole and was only three shots behind, I felt I had a chance."

PUTTING IN THE DARK: "I was too lazy to stand on the practice tee and hit balls, so I used to spend most of my time around the green and in the sand trap. During junior high and high school, on the way home after caddying, we always stopped and putted on one of the greens in the dark. I think that the feel that I developed from putting in the dark helped me develop a very sound putting stroke."

BUFFALO BILL: "I had allergies in the middle 1960s and had to go on a very extensive food rotation program. I needed meat in my diet. There was also elk, moose, bear, and venison. The media caught on to buffalo because of the name association. We capitalized on it and made it my logo. But it led everyone to believe that I ate buffalo day in and day out."

The greatest shot I ever hit would obviously be the 50 foot putt that I hit in the final round of the 1998 Women's US Open. There was an incredible crowd surrounding the green on the 18th hole of Black Wolf Run golf course and the anticipation built as I approached my putt along side my playing partner Liselotte Neumann. Se Ri was in the lead by two, and little did I know she had bogeyed the 17th hole to go to 6-over for the tournament. I was sitting at 7-over but the scoreboard was halted in order to give me the time to putt without the crowd reacting to Se Ri's 17th hole bogey. So as you can imagine, I had no idea what I was getting myself into. I thought for sure that I was just playing for second place and I vividly remember my only concern was not to three-putt!

As my brother Joey and I approached the green, I told him I was so nervous. My brother calmly turned to me and said "I'll read the putt and you just figure out the speed." "Agreed!" I walked down the line of the putt and simply focused on how hard I needed to hit the putt. I got back to my ball and Joey confidently said "Hit it one foot on the left," taking into account the double break of the putt.

Before I knew it, the adrenaline was rushing through my body as I struck the putt as well as I could. It looked great the entire way and before I could gather my thoughts, I shocked myself as the ball entered the cup. Right there on that unforgettable Sunday afternoon, was the best shot I have ever hit!

Jenny Chuasiriporn

Jenny Chuasiriporn

In the 1998 U.S. Women's Open, Jenny Chuasiriporn, a promising 20-year-old amateur from Duke, almost pulled off a major miracle, bowing in a dramatic playoff to South Korea's Se Ri Pak. A year later, she helped lead the Blue Devils to the national championship. A professional career appeared inevitable. But, after failing to qualify for the LPGA Tour, she set out on a different path. Chuasiriporn, 26, runs a program for junior girls in Baltimore.

A WEEK TO REMEMBER: "The Open was really special because I had my family with me. It wasn't very often that they would be able to get out to a tournament. We all stayed in one hotel room, very similar to the way we grew up, which set the tone for the week. My brother, who was on the bag, was the person who guided me into playing well. I couldn't have done it without him."

FAMILY TIES: "My parents gave up so much to have us able to live in the United States. We moved back to Thailand when I was about four, but they decided they had to come back to give their kids the opportunity to do other things. In Thailand, they would have worked nine-to-five jobs, and we would have been normal kids. We wouldn't have been able to access golf as readily as it's available here. I couldn't have gotten the college scholarship."

THE ROAD LESS TRAVELED: "I really enjoy golf on my own terms. I just felt that when I was playing professional golf full-time it really didn't suit me. I was never happy playing every day. I don't regret anything. I would guess that if I hadn't done well at the Open, I probably would have taken more time to relax and figure out what I want to do. I kept going back and forth on it for a couple of years."

JAMES J. COLBERT, JR.

I was playing in the Senior Tournament of Champions at the Hyatt Dorado Beach golf course in Dorado, Puerto Rico in 1995. I was tied with Jim Albus after regulation play. When we got to the first playoff hole, Jim asks me if I want to play for an extra $100. I replied "What, $148,000 isn't enough for you, Jim?" I wanted him to know that we were playing for $148,000 for first place, not a $100. On the first two playoff holes, we each had a chance to beat the other, but no one made the putt. On the third hole, number 18, Albus hits the perfect drive, long and straight. I pushed my drive way off to the right, short and crooked. The ball lands in the fairway bunker. Jim's ball is lying perfect in the fairway and he's looking at a wedge or 9 iron shot. I'm in the fairway bunker with the ball lying close to the front lip, and there's a group of large palm trees between me and the green. I've got to get the ball up over the lip, way out to the right of the trees, hook it back around to the left and carry the bunkers on the right side of the green. I had about 170 yards to go, and I chose a 6 iron. I thought I could get it high enough to get the ball over the lip. I picked the ball perfectly off the sand, and it clears the lip of the bunker. It missed the palm trees to the right and starts to hook; it barely carries over the right hand bunkers, lands about 40 feet short of the hole and heads towards the pin. The ball ended up two feet from the hole. I tap in the putt for the birdie; Jim makes par, and I win the Senior Tournament of Champions. It was the perfect shot at the right time.

Jim Colbert

In his years on the Champions Tour, professional golf's second act, Jim Colbert accomplished what he could not pull off the first time around: He became a star. Colbert, an eight-time winner on the PGA Tour, recorded back-to-back money titles as a senior in 1995 and 1996, and has picked up 20 victories overall. Colbert, 63, who briefly played football in the 1960s at Kansas State, remains one of the program's most enthusiastic boosters.

MY WILDCATS: "I've loved it for 15 years, since Bill Snyder got there and built a top program. The rest of my life, we had to duck. We were terrible. I was 5-foot-9 and not really fast. I had a feel for the game, but separated my shoulder real bad as a freshman and got worried about my golf game. I would have played defensive back, which would have meant tackling a whole bunch of Big Eight fullbacks. I knew there wasn't any future in that."

NO. 1 . . . AT LAST: "It was still a huge accomplishment. I have a poster on my office wall that's framed from an article, which says: 'After 30 years, Colbert is No. 1.' It took me a long time to be No. 1, and yes, it was on the Senior Tour, but it was the same guys I played against my whole life. So it meant a lot to me to be No. 1. Do I wish it had happened on the regular tour? Sure. But it happened later. I just kept sticking my nose in there. I wish I had learned to drive the ball better quicker."

THE HAND WAGGLE: "The first senior tournament I won was in Kansas City. I was on the 17th green on Saturday and made this big, curling, really fast putt. I could have three-putted it in a heartbeat. The cameraman behind the green, as I walked off, jumped from behind the camera and [made the waggle signal] to me, and I responded by doing the exact same thing back to him. When I got to 18, the cameraman did it, and I did it back to him. I had worked as a television commentator with those guys for three years. Every time I did it, I was pointing right at the camera. I do it now because the gallery's always doing it to me."

CHARLES COODY

March 22, 2002

Dear Ron:

Thank you for your patience in my answering your letter regarding the greatest shot that I ever saw plus the best shot that I felt that I was able to hit.

The shot that I most remember seeing someone hit happened when I was a 13-year old boy in 1950 at the Colonial NIT in Fort Worth, Texas. Jerry Barber had hit a second shot over the green on the second hole into a deep rut that had been made by a tire of a truck. After being refused relief from that tire rut, he took some type of wedge, straddled the ball with his back to the hole, hit down on the ball with the club. The ball popped up out of the rut, ran up the slope that was on the back of the green onto the green and down to the hole about six inches from the hole. Even as a 13-year old boy, I realized that I had seen something incredible that had happened because of someone's creative imagination.

As for my own self, considering the circumstances, the best shot I ever made was on the 71st hole of the 1971 Masters. I had slightly hooked my drive up the left side of the 17th fairway, and the ball took a wicked bounce to the left and ran into the front right-hand bunker of the 7th green. I was approximately 150 to 155 yards from the hole with a high lip of the bunker confronting me plus an overhanging pine limb that was sticking out from an adjacent pine tree. I could visually see the flag on the 17th green above the lip of the bunker but below the limb of the pine tree. To this day, I don't know how, but somehow I was able to hit a 7 iron over the lip of the bunker underneath the limb of the pine tree with a slight hook that came to rest just off the right edge of the green about 35 feet from the hole. From there, I had a simple chip and was able to save par and, thus, preserve a 2-shot lead going into the 72nd hole.

Wishing you good success with your project, I remain,

Sincerely yours,

Charles Coody

Charles Coody

During his first eight seasons on the game's center stage in the 1960s, Texas native Charles Coody rarely played the role of leading man. Like many members of the supporting cast, he played in a sport dominated by Jack Nicklaus, Arnold Palmer, Gary Player, Billy Casper, and Lee Trevino. But, in 1971, Coody emerged to win the Masters. Coody, 66, competes on the Champions Tour.

HOGAN HERO: "We didn't have TV then, so all you could rely on was the newspaper. We didn't get golf magazines. When we received the paper in Stamford, which was north of Abilene, we got the *Ft. Worth Star-Telegram,* which had news of Ben Hogan. Hogan had his car wreck in 1949, and I started playing golf in earnest in late 1949 or 1950. I went to Colonial and watched him hit balls."

POLIO: "The kind I had as a kid did not leave me in any type of paralysis. It left me very, very stiff. The first four days I was in the hospital, I had tremendous headaches and a fever. I slept all the time. The only time I would wake up is when they would put hot blankets on me, and this was in the height of the summer. But, on the fifth day, my fever broke, and I felt fine. I was extremely fortunate. There were two others on my block who had it. One was like me. The other became paralyzed from the waist down."

A HALF-PENNY FOR HIS PUTTS: "In 1969, my daughter, Caryn, was with a kid who gave her an English half-penny. The next evening, my wife and I were talking at dinner and I made some reference to the fact that I just couldn't make a putt. Caryn knew I spotted the ball with a coin, so she pulled out this half-penny. 'Here, Daddy, spot the ball with this coin,' she said. 'It will bring you good luck.' I've been spotting my ball with that coin since 1969. I've been lucky not to lose it."

In 1983, at the Canadian Open in Toronto, I arrived at the 72nd hole of regulation tied with Jack Nicklaus. We were 1 stroke behind the leader, Johnny Miller with just the last hole to play. Jack was in the group in front of Johnny and I and he drove the ball in the rough on the 18th hole at Glen Abbey, a 525 yard Par 5. Jack had to lay the ball up to avoid a large lake that protects the right side of the green and the lay up area. I had the honor and striped a drive, right down the left side of the fairway. Johnny pulled his drive to the left and it caught a deep bunker that borders the left side of the fairway.

Jack hit his third shot and left himself with about a 10 ft putt for his birdie. Johnny had to lay up and hit his shot about the same place as Jack had hit his lay up shot. Johnny walked up to his ball as we watched Jack stand over his putt. I am standing back in the fairway, 224 yards away. Just myself and my caddie at the time Dennis Turning (who now caddies for Bruce Fleisher on the Champions Tour) watching the greatest player of all time try to make a putt that would tie him with Johnny.

Dennis kept asking me what I wanted to do, I kept silent about going for it or laying up. As Jack approached his putt, I turned to Dennis and said that we were going to go for it, I could see a smile come to Dennis' face and at that time Jack missed his putt. I then had a second thought and said that we would lay up. You must remember that back in 1983, we didn't hit 5 irons 220 yards and our 1 irons were more like today's 3 iron. My wedge game was pretty good and I thought that I would gave myself a good chance to make birdie from 80 yards.

I could tell Dennis was a bit disappointed as he then had to walk off a lay up yardage. As he was walking back to our ball, I said to forget about it "gimme the 1 iron and let's end this thing!" Dennis said "Damn straight," handed me the 1 iron and backed away so far from the ball that even if I changed my mind again, he wouldn't be able to hear me.

What happened next was the greatest shot of my life came off, a high flying 1 iron that took off right at the hole. The ball hit 10 feet short of the hole, took a peek and continued into the back bunker. An easy up and down that I actually almost made. Johnny hit his approach 12 feet and missed the putt. I tapped in my 6 incher and Johnny and I went into a playoff that I eventually won on the 6th extra hole.

You only have so many chances to beat the greatest in the game and when that opportunity comes along you must grab it. I thought Dennis was going to have a stroke when I told him to get a lay up number but afterwards he said that it was the gutsiest play he had seen and he had previously worked for Tom Kite and David Graham.

John Cook

John Cook

In the summer of 1978, Ohio State's John Cook outdueled Scott Hoch, 5 and 4, to capture the U.S. Amateur. A year later, Cook, a three-time All-American, helped lead the Buckeyes to the NCAA title. Cook, 46, who has worked with former U.S. Open champion Ken Venturi, owns 11 tour victories, including three from his most productive season, 1992. A three-putt on the 71st hole of the British Open at Muirfield that year cost him a great opportunity for a major.

GREATER THAN SCOTT: "The No. 1 amateur at the time was Bobby Clampett, and Scott beat him in the semis. I knew going into the week that I had a good chance. I just had a feeling. I had a week of practice at home completely by myself. Playing Scott, I knew I had to play my best, and I pretty much did that. I made a lot of birdies on a pretty hard golf course. We joke about it a lot. It's hard not to with Scott. He'll always bring up how many putts I made that day."

THE MISTAKE AT MUIRFIELD: "I was playing well and I loved the golf course. I felt like I lost that tournament. I didn't feel like Nick Faldo did anything to win. It was mine. You don't get many chances [to win majors]. I've been close a number of times, but only twice where I actually had a real chance to win, and that was one of them. It was very disappointing, obviously."

ME AND KENNY: "It goes way deeper than golf. He taught me a lot about being responsible for myself in everything. We wouldn't hit that many balls on the range. But, when I was a kid, we played a lot. I wouldn't ask a lot of questions. I would just listen and observe. I believed what he told me. Why wouldn't I? He was one of the great players of his time. He taught me about how to win, what to expect, what your body goes through, and how to adjust."

March 12, 2002

Dear Ron:

The best golf shot I ever hit, given the circumstances, took place on the last hole of 1965 500 Festival Open in Indianapolis, Indiana at Green Tree Country Club.

I was 5 under par leading the tournament when I came to the par 5, 18th hole. Lionel Hebert was in the clubhouse at 4 under, and my playing partner, Jackie Cupit was at 3 under. The hole had a creek running across the fairway just beyond the tee-shot landing area. I hit my drive to the right where it came to rest to the left side of a tree stump, but under a lot of debris and dry leaves. I could identify the ball by bending over, and looking closely, but could not see the ball when standing at address. Cupit knocked his 3 wood second shot onto the green, which was pretty heavily sloped from back to front, and was left with a 20-foot side hill putt for an eagle.

I took a pass at my golf ball, and could only move it a few inches, however I created a path where I could now see my golf ball. I was able to punch my next shot from this position out into the middle of the fairway, short of the creek, some 215 yards from the flagstick.

Given the situation, my 4th shot was, in my mind, the best shot I ever hit. A dead straight 2 iron which finished about 18 inches just below the hole, leaving me a straight uphill putt for par. Cupit missed his eagle putt; I made my putt to win the Tournament.

Apart from seeing several hole-in one shots, the best shot I ever saw was on the 71st hole of the US Open at Pebble Beach in 1972, when Jack Nichlaus hit his one iron stiff, and went on the win the Championship. I finished 3 shots back in second place.

Wishing you well with your project, I extend kindest regards.

Respectfully,

Bruce Crampton

Bruce Crampton

Bruce Crampton made the long pilgrimage from Down Under to America in the late 1950s. He earned 14 victories on the regular tour and 20 as a senior. Crampton rarely took a break, once teeing it up 38 tournaments in a row. Four times he came close to winning a major, but, on each occasion, he finished second to Jack Nicklaus. Crampton, 68, runs Bruce Crampton's Sports Performance, LLC, in Annapolis, Maryland.

JACK OF ALL SECONDS: "He was the best player in the world at that time, and if you can't win, it's nice to be second. I was the defending runner-up in those championships the following year. I think I should have won the U.S. Open at Pebble Beach in 1972. On the 10th hole of the last day, I was playing ahead of Jack, and nailed it with a driver; it was into the wind. I hit it so solidly that it did not kick down the hill away from the fairway bunker. Instead, it bounced straight forward into the fairway bunker. I made a double bogey. Behind me, Jack hit it into the ocean. And then, on 14, I was playing with Kermit Zarley, who hit his third shot over the back of the green under the television tower. I had to wait for him to take a drop. It took forever, and my hands got cold. I three-putted."

IRONMAN: I wasn't living over here at the time, so I couldn't commute back and forth to Australia the way the players do now. What people didn't know was that the clubs would go in the boot of the car when I got to the airport in Sydney, and sometimes they wouldn't come out again for six or eight weeks because I was completely fed up with golf by the time I played that many tournaments."

KNOW WHEN TO FOLD 'EM: "I said that I would always walk away from it [professional golf] when I didn't feel like I could be really competitive anymore. When you've done something reasonably well and you know what that feels like, anything less than that gets frustrating. I have a lot of pride."

BEN D. CRENSHAW

August 18, 2003

Dear Michael:

The best shot I ever hit was a left-handed nine iron on the par-5, 13th hole at Warwick Hills Country Club in Grand Blanc, Michigan during the final round of the 1986 Buick Open. It was a desperate shot, the only one I could play.

After hooking my second shot, a dreadful four iron, my ball ended up about 30 yards left of the green, directly under a spruce tree. Hitting it right-handed was out of the question, as I was stymied with a right-handed swing. I knew I had to keep pace with the other players on the leader board and par wouldn't be good enough at this stage.

I decided to turn the club upside down and swing left-handed. It was certainly not the kind of shot one ever thinks of practicing. The only good thing in my favor was that the ball was sitting up fairly nice. I caught it solid, and the ball ended up about six feet from the hole! Frankly, I would have been satisfied with anything up towards the green.

It gave me the boost I needed. I made the putt for birdie and went on to win the tournament by a single shot.

With sincere best wishes,

Ben D. Crenshaw

Ben Crenshaw

For all the magnificent putts that Ben Crenshaw has converted, it was one of the shortest ones—18 inches on the 72nd hole of the 1995 Masters—that stands out. Few will forget the sight of Crenshaw, who had lost his longtime mentor, Harvey Penick, only days earlier, breaking down after the ball fell into the cup. In 1999, he served as captain of the victorious U.S. Ryder Cup squad at Brookline. Crenshaw, 52, plays on the Champions Tour and designs golf courses.

THE BEST WITH THE BLADE: "I never got to see Bobby Locke, but I would say it was a toss-up between Billy Casper and Dave Stockton and Tom Watson in his heyday. Each had entirely different styles. When I talk to people about putting, I go back to what Harvey said a long time ago to all of us when we were growing up, that we had to cultivate our own style. Each person gets comfortable over the ball in a different way. He always implored us not to look like anyone else when we were putting. But, if I had to pick one player to make one putt, it would be Jack Nicklaus."

FAVORITE GOLF BOOKS: "I am absolutely enthralled with *Bobby Jones On Golf.* It is an instruction book, but there is so much about the mental side of golf and what a golfer feels like when they go through a swing. It's incredible how that book is put together. There is one beautiful little essay after another about different facets of the game. I have never seen anything put together that fluently. It's not a book for experts, although it talks about people who play the game on a high level. It gives thoughts to middle handicappers and to people who are just starting the game."

NO HOME ON THE RANGE: "I didn't enjoy practicing. I don't now. I have not been able to keep my concentration a long time on a practice tee. I love to play. I practice when I play. I'll hit three balls on a hole if nobody's around. It's more realistic to me. I'm playing all the shots. I've had many times in my career where I've forced myself to hit balls, and I go backwards a lot of times."

ROBERTO DE VICENZO

BUENOS AIRES, ARGENTINA

27 August 2002

Dear Ron:

Thinking back on my competitive career, which began when
I became a professional at the age of fiteen in 1938, I
can't pinpoint one favorite shot in particular--but I do
remember some double-eagles that I enjoyed: a driver and
2-iron on the 17th hole at Muirfield; a driver and 3-wood
on the 14th hole during the Jamaica Open; a driver and
4-wood on the 7th hole at Ranelagh in the Argentina Open.

I've also had 17 holes-in-one, including one in a tournament
in Florida where the prize was a beautiful American car.
Because of import restrictions, unfortunately, I couldn't
take it back to Argentina--¡qué lástima!

I always thought the best possible shot in golf would be
a hole-in-one on a par five, perhaps on a horseshoe-shaped
hole where one could hit over some trees and find the green.
Now that I'm getting older and hitting shorter, I'm forced
to admit that such a feat has escaped me. Perhaps one of
today's strong young pros will accomplish it one day.

Since I played tournament golf for so many decades, I had the
honor of playing with all the great names of the past century's
second half. Of course I saw the masters of the game make many
memorable shots, but I particularly remember a remarkable shot
made by my playing partner, Lee Trevino. We were on the par-
three 17th hole at Pebble Beach, with the wind blowing so hard
against us that we could hardly keep our balance standing on
the tee. Lee hit a driver into that wind and left it a foot
from the hole. I'm still impressed.

Thank you for including me in your project, Ron. I look
forward to playing golf with you next time I'm in California.

                              Sincerely,

                              Roberto De Vicenzo

Roberto De Vicenzo

Argentine star Roberto De Vicenzo, 81, picked up more than 200 titles around the world, including the 1967 British Open, but it was the way he lost the 1968 Masters that will forever define his exceptional career. De Vicenzo was headed for an 18-hole playoff with Bob Goalby when he signed an incorrect scorecard. De Vicenzo was inducted into the World Golf Hall of Fame in 1989.

Roberto De Vicenzo wasn't the only professional golfer to make a mistake at the worst possible moment. Following are golfers who were disqualified for a rule violation:

1957 U.S. WOMEN'S OPEN: Jackie Pung was the apparent victor on the East Course at Winged Foot outside New York City until it was learned that she signed for a 5 instead of a 6 at the par-5, fourth hole. While her total for the round was accurate, giving her the win, Pung was disqualified for signing an incorrect scorecard. Club members and writers took up a collection that raised about $3,000 in cash, nearly double the amount of the first-place check. Pung, 82, gives lessons in Hawaii.

1966 PENSACOLA OPEN: At the halfway mark, the colorful Doug Sanders enjoyed a comfortable four-stroke advantage. Too comfortable, it seems. Sanders forgot to sign his card, instead signing dozens of autographs. "It was like being hit in the head with a stick," Sanders recalled last year. "A rule is a rule, and that's life."

1987 ANDY WILLIAMS OPEN: On the 14th hole in the third round at Torrey Pines Golf Course in La Jolla, California, Craig Stadler knelt on a towel to hit a ball from under a tree. He didn't want to stain his slacks. The next day, a replay was shown on the air, prompting a viewer to call in and say that Stadler broke the rules. Officials decided that he built an illegal stance, incurring an automatic two-stroke penalty. Stadler was disqualified for signing an incorrect scorecard, depriving him of second place and $37,333.

Dear Michael:

Golf is a stressful sport, an exhilarating sport, and a tearful sport. I experienced all of these emotions one day in April 1974. It was a day I will never forget, as that one shot put me in the history books and gave me a career that I cherish.

I qualified for the PGA Tour in 1967, and was in the Top 60 money winners in 1968. That year, I was in an historic playoff with Jack Nicklaus at Firestone Country Club in Akron, finally losing on the fifth extra hole. I knew I was close to winning my first tournament, but victory kept eluding me.

Then came that day at Pensacola Country Club in Pensacola, Florida. Entering the last hole on Sunday afternoon, I was a shot behind Peter Oosterhuis. The tournament was the Monsanto Open. My tee shot at 18 went left. From 164 yards out, I was faced with a most difficult hook shot, blocked out by trees. It was the only shot I had to reach the green. I pulled it off with a six iron, executing just the right amount of hook to get the ball about eight feet from the pin. I made the putt for the birdie, getting into the playoff with Oosterhuis, who I defeated on the fourth hole when I sunk a 15-footer.

I was so excited, I literally jumped three feet off the ground. With the win, I was going to play in the 1975 Masters, the first African-American to receive that opportunity! I was, however, taken off the course at Pensacola in a hurry. There had been, I found out, numerous death threats against me.

There was one sight I will never forget. A little girl, maybe nine years old, had greeted me at the course earlier that morning. She gave me a large sign that stated: "All things are possible for he who Believeth." I carried that thought with me for the rest of day—and for the rest of my life. Golf is, indeed, a privilege to play.

Lee Elder

Lee Elder

The contribution Lee Elder made to the game can't be measured in conventional terms. Elder was a pioneer. In 1975, he became the first black golfer to appear in the Masters, a tremendously symbolic moment in a white-dominated sport. It was not the first time he broke an important barrier. Four years earlier, he played golf in South Africa. Elder, 69, won four events on the PGA Tour, eight on the senior circuit.

YOU TALK ABOUT PRESSURE: "I was nervous on the first tee in the 1975 Masters. The one thing that calmed me down was the fact that I played with a man I admired and became close with, Gene Littler. He said, 'Relax, be yourself. Relax as much as you possibly can.' That first tee shot was the hardest shot that I've hit in my life. There was so much riding on it. I didn't want to be embarrassed. I could just picture myself topping the ball or hitting one of those big slices into the woods on the right. It split the center of the fairway, and I then hit an 8 iron to about 15 feet right of the flag."

SOUTH AFRICA: "I was trying to do something to help a pretty bad situation. I was also doing a favor for Gary Player, who had been pickcted here, people shouting obscenities at him. My advisers told me that we did not want to make the mistake of going directly from the United States to South Africa. So, as a goodwill ambassador, I went to all the black African countries before I took the trip to South Africa."

DUELING JACK: "I had a couple of chances to win [the 1968 American Golf Classic], especially on the second playoff hole when Jack Nicklaus hit it in the bunker. I thought I had him on the run. A victory would have gotten me more relaxed; I would have won more tournaments early in my career. But [the performance] let me know that I had the game to play with the top players. Firestone was one of the toughest golf courses that we played at the time."

My most memorable shot was actually a putt! In 1995 at the PGA Championship at the famed Riviera Country Club, I needed a career round to make the Ryder Cup Team. I was outside the top 10 on the points list and needed a top 5 finish in the tournament. Starting in 21st on Sunday morning, I came to the 18th 8 under for the day. After a solid tee shot and poor iron, my chip shot rolled 12 feet by the cup. The greens were inconsistent with spike marks everywhere. I needed to split 2 spike marks to make the putt. I hit one of the most beautiful putts of my career at the most crucial time and shot 63 to make the team!

Brad Faxon

Since his first full year on the PGA Tour in 1984, Rhode Island's Brad Faxon, 42, has finished in the Top 90 on the money list every season with only one exception. Faxon, a supreme putter, has won seven tournaments and participated on two U.S. Ryder Cup squads (1995, 1997). Along with childhood buddy and fellow tour veteran Billy Andrade, Faxon hosts an annual tournament for charity.

DAD AND THE KING: "My dad caddied for me in the last round of the 1983 U.S. Open at Oakmont after a college friend had to go back to school. Paired with D. A. Weibring, the thing I remember most about that day was after we hit our drives on 15. At about the same time, Arnold Palmer, who was playing 18, had hooked his drive into the fairway bunker by the 15th tee. After walking about 200 yards, I noticed that my dad was still by the bunker, watching Palmer play. It was very funny. 'I've never been that close to Arnold Palmer,' he said when he caught up to us."

FRIENDS FOREVER: "Billy and I go way back. We've always been competitors and friends, pushing ourselves, pushing each other. He was a better national-level player, and I was better on the state level. It's hard to overestimate how good it's been to have a close friend do what I do, to compare notes, to practice together, to inspire each other. In 1991, when I won the Buick tournament in Michigan, he was on his way to the airport. He changed his flight and turned around to celebrate the night with me."

TRY NOT TO CARE: "It always amazes me when people think I'm lucky to be a good putter. I've worked at it over and over. People ask me all the time for the key, and the thing I tell them that's most important is to throw away the fear. Can you putt as if you don't care if you miss? Because, if you can, you'll putt better. Why do you always hit a mulligan better than the first one? Because you don't care. It's not easy. It takes practice and positive thoughts. But it can be done."

David Feherty

Northern Ireland's David Feherty, 45, has been a huge hit since he made the move to television in the mid-1990s, blending insightful analysis with a refreshing wit. Feherty has also written several books and contributes a monthly column to Golf Magazine. A member of Europe's Ryder Cup team in 1991, he was a five-time champion on the European Tour and finished second in the 1994 New England Classic.

SILENCE IS GOLDEN: "CBS was looking for someone at about the time that Ben Wright was let go, and I just happened to be on this side of the Atlantic with not a whole lot to do. I had dreamt about it for a long time. If CBS hadn't come around, I would have found my way into some seedy television [gig] or even seedier department of a newspaper. I don't think there is anywhere near enough silence on television today. A lot of people I talk to turn the sound down, and I don't blame them. Everybody has something to say, and everybody has to say it. Sometimes, you just say, 'Here it is, for birdie and the lead,' and you shut up for 30 or 40 seconds and let the tension build. Nothing builds tension like silence."

COPING WITH HATRED: "People always joked about the stuff that was going on in Northern Ireland. That's how you survive, whether it's the Warsaw Ghetto or the Middle East. How do they laugh? It's self-defense. Nothing else can seem serious after that. I can't watch the story of a child abduction without basically being moved to tears. I have a tremendous ability to empathize or put myself where someone else is. There will be no solution while they teach history. There will be lulls, but while our parents teach us to hate somebody, there's no chance."

PAYNE TO THE RESCUE: "I was four up with four to play [in the Ryder Cup] and had lost a couple of holes. Payne had to help me get onto the tee because this giant lady marshal thought I was a spectator, and this is when he was supposed to be a [jerk], which he never was. 'Where in the hell do you think you're going?' she said, blocking me from getting to the tee. He put his arm around me and said: 'He's playing against me,' and swept me up to the tee."

Dear Ron,

Sorry it has taken me so long for me to reply, but McCord made me write replies to both fan letters he received this year before he let me out from under his desk.

It was the final of the 1990 Dunhill Cup, which was in effect the three-man team championship of the world and yours truly was, through no fault of my own, the gallant skipper of the Irish side. My two teammates were Ronan Rafferty and Philip Walton, and we were up against the old enemy, the English.

The event was played in October over the hallowed turf of the Old Course at St. Andrews, and I'll be damned if I can remember which teams had the decency to lose to us on our way to the final, but I'm fairly sure some of them must have been communists. As captain, I had chosen to play in the last of the three matches and was drawn against my friend, the veteran Ryder Cupper and formidable match player, Howard Clark. That day I teed off with what Saddam Hussein might have called, "The Mother of All Hangovers," and had it not been for the kindness/bigotry of the Scottish spectators, it was a match I surely would have lost. You have to understand that after the Scots are knocked out of any team event in any sport, they will instantly become rabid supporters of anyone who is playing the English. That's just the way it works.

Now as I mentioned, I wasn't feeling exactly spiffing, and subsequently, after a dozen or so holes of medal/match play, some blundering, and one near fall into one of the Coffins, I found myself a couple back of Howard. Trust me, in professional golf, there is no worse feeling than hitting a three-foot putt so fat that the bastard finishes short of the hole. But then, as I made my way from one green to the next tee, in an Elijah-and-the-chariot-of-fire-descending-from-the-heavens kind of way, a shiftless, tweedy-looking sort in the crowd made contact with me.

Don't ask me where it happened, because I can't remember. St. Andrews is a magnificent enough illusion at the best of times, but when you can't tell whether you're blown up or stuffed, it's like a day-trip into golf's hall of mirrors. (By the way, I've always wanted to rename the hazards at St. Andrews. Screw the principal, and his nose too. I mean, what kind of a nose has only one nostril?)

"Hey, Jimmy!" this idiot hissed [for that is the customary way to hail a stranger in Scotland]. "Ye look like ye might need a wee biff on the magic bongwater!"

I glanced over at this crumpled overcoat of a man with his impossibly small head, crowned by, of all things, an Oakland A's baseball cap. With skeletal fingers, the wee man was clutching a dirty pewter hip flask to his chest, as if it contained a genie of some kind. He was grinning broadly, displaying a mouth full of broken china, and his eyes were closer together than a racing dog's balls. The right shoulder of his coat was shiny and worn, so instantly I knew he was a caddie, and a lifer at that.

"Aye, go awan," said the gormless pal, who had a face like a half-chewed caramel, looked equally fit, and had the demeanor of someone who might just have a betting slip favoring the Micks about his dingy person.

I stopped, and hesitated for about a millisecond, which was about an hour longer than needed to get the crowd involved. I was going to look like a fairy if I didn't take a hit on the flask. Accompanied by a few hoots, at least one holler, and an indeterminate number of slaps on the back, I threw a good swallow down my neck and spent the next few minutes trying to cough up an internal organ. In certain parts of Scotland, the locals still make their own firewater, which is then covertly distributed in unlabeled whiskey bottles. (They don't have to tear off the old label, because as soon as the bottle is refilled, it jumps off by itself.)

I don't know what the stuff was, maybe some kind of industrial cleaning product, but I couldn't speak for about four holes. It had the unfortunate side effect of making the entire golf course seem somewhat mauve, but boy did it straighten me up. I played like a man possessed, and by the time I'd signed my scorecard, I'd halved the match, and the final was tied. To decide it, Howard and I had to play a sudden-death playoff.

My two caddie pals were waiting for me at the edge of the practice green before I teed off, and once more I felt it best to comply with their instructions. After all, they seemed to know how to get a man around St. Andrews. Howard and I halved the first two holes, but as fate would have it, this trip would end on the next, the legendary Road Hole.

I stood on the tee, gazing at the building in front of me with its famous lettering emblazoned across the wall, "Old Course Hotel." I hadn't a clue what line to hit my tee shot on, and was waiting for the ground to stop moving so I could tee up my ball, when, sensing my confusion Harry, my faithful sack-dragger, muttered out of the corner of his mouth, "Hit it at the 'F' in Hotel."

"Harry," I said, "there is no 'F' in Hotel."

Harry looked at the ground, shaking his head. "No, no, no, you idiot," he hissed under his breath. "I said hit it at the EFFING hotel."

"Oh yeah," I nodded. "I thought that's what you meant."

So I hit it at the effing hotel, and the right-to-left wind drifted the ball back to the left edge of the fairway. Howard missed the fairway left, then pulled his second way left of the green, leaving his ball with one of the world's most impossible chip shots, from behind the ghastly little toilet bowl known as the Road Bunker. This was my chance. One good swing, a high draw with a 3-iron, land the ball on the little nasal outcrop at the front of the green/mauve, and let it run up toward the back lip, and hope the slope takes it around behind the hole.

I'd love to say I remember the swing, but I don't. I swung, it flew, and suddenly it got deafeningly quiet in my head. I do, however, have a lasting image of the ball, hung up in a sepia sky, drifting past the cherry-picker camera and descending dream-like down in front of the backdrop of the crowd in the bleachers behind the road. As the ball landed on the front of the green, people began to stand up. Carried back to me by the breeze, the roar began to build, and the silence was gone.

Like the undertow from a Mexican wave, the crowd noise sucked the ball toward the back edge of the green, perilously close to the little lip over which lies the tarmac road and the dreaded limestone wall, and then it gently blew my little egg back down and around behind the flagstick, where it nestled about 15 feet from the hole. Two putts from there, and I had won the Dunhill Cup for Ireland, on the most famous hole on the most famous course in the world.

Jack Fleck & Associates
GOLF COURSE ARCHITECTURE

— ARCHITECTS —
Jack Fleck
U.S. OPEN WINNER
Pete Fleck
LANDSCAPE ARCHITECT

March 22, 2003

Dear Dr. Cherney:

My greatest and most important shot was on the 72nd hole of the 1955 United States Open Golf Championship at the Olympic Club in San Francisco, California.

After hitting my 3 wood off the tee, to about 5 or 6 inchs in the first cut of rough, on a slightly up slope and a beautiful lie.

It was about 130 yards uphill and just over the front bunker to the hole, on the front right side of the green.

I felt a full 8 iron would not stop close to the hole, as I needed to make a birdie 3 to tie Hogan for the Championship at 287.

I made the slight down hill putt that had a inch right to left break, which tied Ben Hogan, who finished 2 hours beforehand.

I was fortunate to be able to hit my high soft 7 iron that close to the 72nd hole. I was in the second to last twosome of the final 36 holes of play. They told me after I tied Hogan, that the TV went off the air when I was on the 71st hole, declaring that Hogan won his 5th United States Open Golf Championship.

Wishing you the best, Sincerely,

Jack Fleck

Jack Fleck

Searching for perhaps the biggest shocker in the history of the major championships? Well, search no further than the remarkable story of Jack Fleck, an ex-caddie, who outdueled the legendary Ben Hogan in an 18-hole playoff to capture the 1955 U.S. Open at The Olympic Club in San Francisco. Prior to that week, the best Fleck had finished was fifth at the 1949 Cedar Rapids Open. Fleck, 82, won two more tournaments and achieved moderate success on the Senior Tour.

BEATING BIG BEN: "I remember it like it was yesterday. About two or three weeks later, when we were having lunch, Jerry Barber, who I played a lot of golf with, said, 'Jack, I knew you were the only guy who could beat Ben Hogan head-to-head in the playoff.' He [Hogan] always treated me well. A lot of the old-time pros on tour said, 'I bet he hates your guts.' He never treated me that way."

PUTS DOWN PUTTING: "I should have had a better career, but I was always a terrible putter. You don't win unless you putt real well. I would've won an awful lot of tournaments. I've always thought too much of a premium was put on putting. A putt hangs on the lip and you hit it a quarter of an inch, and that's equal to a good drive or a good wedge. Anytime you're on the putting surface, it should only be half a stroke per time you stroke the ball. That will equalize who is the greatest player."

GOING FOR THE GOLD: "I only won $6,000 for the Open victory. Now they win a million. So you had to make money on exhibitions and outings. It drew you away from continually playing in tournaments. It wasn't till around 1959 that I started playing better again."

March 27, 2002

Dear Ron,

The Greatest Golf Shot I Ever Hit
By: Raymond Floyd

In 1981, I had one of my best years ever on tour. I won five tournaments and had eighteen top 10 finishes. However, heading into the 1982 Memorial Tournament in May, I still had not won an event that year. At The Memorial, I played well the first three days and was in a great position to win the event when I reached the par five 11th hole. I drove the ball poorly, leaving myself under the lip of the fairway bunker. Since I couldn't hit the ball over the lip of the bunker and over the creek that crossed the center of the fairway, I laid up with a sand wedge. Unfortunately, I didn't get the ball as far up as I would have liked. I figured I had to lay up again and try to wedge it close to save my par. I asked my caddy "Golf Ball" how far I needed to hit it to lay up short of the green. He replied, "Come on, man. You can knock it on that green. You've only got 235." At that time, I carried my three-wood exactly 235 yards but the green is slightly elevated and there's a creek short of the green. I told "Golf Ball" that I could still make par by laying up short but he was adamant that I try to knock it on. I decided to trust him. I pulled out my three-wood and hit it perfect. The ball stopped in the middle of the green, and I made an easy par. After making two more birdies down the stretch, I had won the Memorial Tournament. The shot I hit on 11 jump-started my year. I won two more events that year including my second PGA Championship in August.

The Greatest Shot I Ever Saw
By: Raymond Floyd

The best shot I ever saw was Tom Watson's chip in on the 71st hole of the 1982 US Open at Pebble Beach. Based upon the difficulty of the shot and the situation Watson was in, that was certainly one of the greatest shots of all-time and the greatest one I ever witnessed.

I wish you all the best with the book. I eagerly anticipate sitting down and reading it.

Sincerely,

Raymond Floyd

Raymond Floyd

Except for the cherished Claret Jug, Raymond Floyd has acquired the grand prizes in his profession: two PGA Championships (1969, 1982), a Masters crown (1976), and a U.S. Open triumph at Shinnecock Hills (1986). A frequent Ryder Cup participant, Floyd was inducted into the World Golf Hall of Fame in 1989. Floyd, 61, has 22 victories overall and 14 as a senior.

BETTER LATE THAN . . . : "I knew [in 1986] I wasn't going to have a lot of chances left. I played very well the week before in Westchester, and then shot 77 in the last round. That might have been the thing that got me over the hump because Maria [his wife] pressed the issue, driving out from Westchester to South Hampton on Sunday night: 'What happens if you get in contention? You've got to address why things went wrong.' She made me address it. It got my psyche and my focus and my vision so much more acute."

THE STARE: "I read in the newspaper, or I used to read, that another player said, 'He's so intimidating.' You know I never considered myself an intimidator on the golf course. I always felt I was a comfortable guy to play with. I complimented people on good shots, and tried to conduct myself like a gentleman on the course. If I could self-induce that stare, I would have won a lot more. Maria said, 'I've seen him win without the look, but I have never seen him lose with it.'"

THE CUBBIES: "I met Leo [Durocher, their future manager] in 1964 when he was a coach with the Dodgers. I lived in Chicago from 1969 to 1973, and traveled with that '69 team that blew it at the end to the Mets. I had a locker in the clubhouse for many years. I grew up in North Carolina, and our team was the St. Louis Cardinals. I used to lay in my bed with the radio on KMOX and my parents didn't know it. Now I'm a huge Cubs fan. Who is our most wanted enemy? The St. Louis Cardinals."

Dear Michael,

As a young boy my father encouraged me to play the game. Living about 10 miles from the closest golf course we dug holes in our lawn at home and that was our putting green. He would also dump a truckload of sand to the side, so I could practice bunker shots. Needless to say I love the sand.

USF&G 1999 New Orleans 72nd hole. I have to get up and down to make a playoff with Greg Norman, who is already in the clubhouse. The shot is about 80 feet long. I step into the bunker to feel my lie (with my feet) before I walk onto the green for a pitch mark whereupon something goes through my mind. "If I land the shot about here, it can go in the hole." This spot is about 15-20 feet from the hole, with the bunker being quite firm the ball would roll about that much. I walk back to my ball, line it up and try to aim around about that spot on the green.

The ball comes out of the trap as planned and runs smoothly in the hole. I win.

Sincerely,

David Frost

David Frost

The underrated David Frost has collected 10 victories since he earned his playing privileges in the mid-1980s. His playoff triumph over Ben Crenshaw in the 1989 World Series of Golf provided him with the much-coveted 10-year tour exemption. Frost, 44, operates a 300-acre vineyard in the wine-producing region of his native South Africa.

VERY GOOD YEAR: "I was never the farm boy; my brother was. I've always known when the weather's been good for the vintage and when the grapes need to be picked. It's been in my blood, I guess. I grew up in a vineyard. My dad had a vineyard and my grandfather had a vineyard. I used to hit golf balls in the vineyards. The last seven or eight years is when I really got interested in wine. I've learned a lot from other connoisseurs. More of a French style is what I like."

A GAME FOR ANIMALS: "From the age of 4 or 5 years old, everyone in South Africa knows rugby. I was on rugby teams until I was 16 years old. It was your life. They say rugby is a game for animals that humans play. At the level I played, kids don't get hurt that much. I think it's of great importance to play a team sport, even if, later on, you're going to perform as an individual. You need to be able to recognize the fact you've got people around you all the time. It takes a lot of pressure off of you, to be able to relax and not focus on yourself all the time."

THE RIGHT TIME: "I never thought I was good enough to do what I ended up doing. I never had huge expectations, and, as I kept playing, things developed. My whole life has been like that. I started playing at 12. I don't think it's that good to start at a really young age because you're too young to master the mechanics of the swing. You are better off starting later properly than starting younger wrong. There are players who have turned pro too young."

Sergio Garcia
Club de Campo del Mediterráneo

Dear Michael:

In 1982, at the age of two in Spain, I choked up on the club and hit this incredible drive...No, no, just kidding. My best shot was one that I'm sure a lot of people remember, on the 16th hole at Medinah in the final round of the 1999 PGA. I hit my three wood from the tee a bit too straight, sending my ball toward the trees. I didn't think it would be too much of a problem, until I got closer. The ball was in a bad lie, right next to the roots. 'Geez, what am I going to do now?' I thought.

One thing I wasn't going to do was play it safe by chipping out into the fairway. Maybe if I were out of contention, I might decide to do that, but I was only a couple shots behind Tiger, a chance to win a major. To have a good possibility of making par, I had to go for it. The risk seemed worth it.

I was 186 from the green. I grabbed my five iron, but then changed to a six, seeing a five was too much club. With the face wide open, I aimed about 30 yards left of the green, hoping to slice it as much as I could. Even if I didn't slice it enough, I figured I could still get up and down to make four.

As I swung, I closed my eyes, too scared to look at what might happen if I missed the ball by a fraction of an inch. But, after impact, I quickly opened them, and saw the ball going on a good line towards the left side of the green. I started to run down the fairway because, from my angle, there was a slope in front of me. I wanted to see where the ball ended up. It ended up 60 feet from the pin, and I two-putted for par. I didn't win the PGA that day, but I sure gave it my best try.

Sergio García,

Sergio Garcia

Spain's Sergio Garcia turned pro at the age of 19 and has been a major attraction ever since. In August 1999, he almost became a major winner, dueling with Tiger Woods down to the last hole of the PGA Championship at Medinah. A two-time Ryder Cup participant, Garcia has won three tournaments in the United States and four on the European Tour. In 2002, Garcia, 24, finished in the Top 10 of all four majors.

Fans will not soon forget the drama that unfolded at the 16th hole that Sunday at Medinah—both the shot and the sprint. Nor will the announcing crew at CBS. Following are some of their reflections:

"I was 15 feet away. Immediately after he made the run up the fairway and the leap, he walked over to me on the left side of the fairway. He took my hand and put it on his chest, right above his heart. He goes, 'Feel this.' His heartbeat was 150 beats a second. I turned to him, and I said, 'Sergio, I have a feeling that this is just one of many times you're going to feel that kind of a heartbeat in your career,' and he laughed."—*Peter Kostis*

"I would have given him 100 balls and he couldn't hit it on the green three times. As flamboyant and aggressive as he is, you knew that if there was any hope, a 10 percent hope, that he would try it. You just knew it."—*Gary McCord*

"One of the great clutch shots that we've seen in the modern era. It didn't lead to a win, but that was a guy making something out of nothing."—*Jim Nantz*

Feb 15 2002

Dear Ron

The best shot I ever hit was in the 1968 Masters on the par 5 15th hole final round. I hit a three iron that ended 6½ feet from the pin and the green was very firm (hard) I made the putt for an eagle three and went on to win the tournament by 1 shot.

Bobby Jones, the president of the Augusta National golf club wrote me a letter after the Masters and said the 3 iron shot was the finest long iron he had ever seen Played to the 15th hole. He said he didn't see Gene Sarazens shot for a double eagle in 1935.

Sincerely,
Bob Goalby

GOLF COURSE DESIGN

BOB GOALBY   KYE GOALBY

Bob Goalby

In April 1968, Bob Goalby put on a green jacket, joining an exclusive club of Masters champions. Goalby, who benefited from Roberto De Vicenzo's unforgettable blunder, was an outstanding player. The tour's Rookie of the Year in 1958, he finished with 11 victories and was a member of the 1963 U.S. Ryder Cup team. After his playing days ended, Goalby, 75, went to work for NBC.

A BAD RAP: "I was friends with Roberto before that and after that. That didn't change our friendship. He was mad at himself. It was unfortunate for him, but it was also unfortunate for me. I shot the fourth-lowest [four-round] score that had ever been shot there and I didn't get credit for the tournament. I got 500 letters saying that I was the worst son of a bitch who ever lived. The articles were a joke. None of them had the facts. They thought I played with him."

PLAYING FOR UNCLE SAM: "Whenever you represent your country, whether it was 1929 or 2002, it was still exciting. Those guys who play now act like nobody else ever played in the Ryder Cup. I would have been on the 1961 Ryder Cup team, but you had to be a pro for five years and I was one month shy of five years. I was third on the points list."

EIGHT WAS ENOUGH: "It was on my birthday in 1961, the final round of the St. Petersburg Open, when I made eight straight birdies. I was trailing by one when I teed off and by two at the sixth hole. I birdied No. 8 from about 15 feet, and two-putted from the fringe for another birdie on the ninth, a par 5. On the next hole, I hit an eight iron about two feet from the hole. I made five more in a row after that. Going for nine straight, I hit an eight iron that went past the hole about 20 feet. I didn't come close to making it. I wound up winning by five."

Natalie Gulbis

At age 14 I was then the youngest to qualify for an LPGA event. I Monday morning qualified for the Longs Drug Challenge in my hometown Sacramento, CA. As I approached what would be my final hole of the event, the par 4- 18th Hole at Twelve Bridges Golf Club requires a demanding drive with a tough second shot to a elevated green. After hitting a perfect drive down the center, I fired a mid iron at the pin leaving a 10-foot uphill put for Birdie. The cheers from the crowds could be heard for miles; I walked up to the green with a standing ovation. The rush of adrenaline confirmed that my dream to play professional golf was with in my reach. My hometown fans cheered again after sinking my putt for birdie. I fulfilled my dream 4 years later when I earned my LPGA tour card at age 18.

Natalie Gulbis

Natalie Gulbis

After one year at the University of Arizona, Natalie Gulbis skipped a few grades—all the way to the LPGA Tour. In 2002, she finished second to Beth Bauer in the race for Rookie of the Year, with more than $250,000 in earnings. A former gymnast, Gulbis has made an important contribution to a tour in search of young stars. Gulbis, 21, started playing golf at the age of four.

HELLO, WORLD: "The whole week was a blur. I qualified on Monday and [got to the tournament] on Tuesday. I was at the golf course for eight hours and was at the practice tee for only 20 minutes, maybe a half hour. I spent the whole day doing interviews. The media just blew me away. I finally got to catch my breath when I teed off on the first hole. I hit it right down the center. I wasn't nervous. Gymnastics took a lot of my nerves out of it. I didn't play in another LPGA event till the U.S Open after my year at Arizona. I birdied my first two holes, looked at the leaderboard, and saw my name up there. I turned professional after that event. I wanted to be there."

OLGA WHO?: "I wasn't that good. I was competitive for probably four or five years. I did all four events and got to a level 8, two levels below level 10, which is where the Olympic gymnasts are at. I was a little too tall, and my golf was going forward so fast. My parents were worried about me getting hurt. It's a lot easier to make a four- or five-foot putt than to land a dismount off the bars."

READING LINES, NOT PUTTS: "Three nights a week, for a couple of hours, I took classes with Howard Fine, one of the top two or three acting coaches in L.A. You started from the basics. It was like being with Butch Harmon, exciting and interesting. It came up that I would have some opportunities to be on a couple of shows, but it would not have fit in well with being a professional athlete."

GOLF SERVICES, INC.

Hale Irwin
President

March 31, 2003

Dear Michael,

   The greatest shot I ever hit: In 1974 at the U.S. Open at Winged Foot I was playing the 72nd hole nursing what was a precarious two-shot lead. The 18th hole was a difficult driving hole worsened by a very demanding second shot. The rough was indescribably treacherous, and the green was elevated and undulating with an extremely quick putting surface.

   Fortunately, I hit my drive into the fairway. Now, facing a 194 yard shot, slightly uphill, and a breeze blowing left to right, I chose a 2-iron. The shot was nearly perfect as I trusted my mechanics and my belief that I could play the shot successfully under the pressure of the U.S. Open. A mis-hit could lead to an easy bogey or worse. Upon contact with the ball I knew I had hit it well. The trajectory was perfect, slightly left of the flag and let the wind blow it in to the flagstick. The ball came down quite near to the hole and rolled some 20-25 feet past the cup. A two-putt from there gave me my first U. S. Open victory.

   The greatest shot I ever witnessed by another player: The second hole at Augusta National provided me a glimpse of what made Jack Nicklaus so great. His tee shot came to rest in the fairway some 230 yards from the green. A downhill lie complicated by the ball being above his feet and the large pine tree growing over the left side of the green gave me pause to wonder what he would do. The answer was a 1-iron played right over the top of the flag coming to rest on the back fringe of the left side of the green. Surely from that distance with that lie and the height required to get over the tree it should not be attempted, much less be done! Nicklaus achieved it and it made for the best shot I have ever witnessed.

Sincerely,

Hale Irwin

Hale Irwin

Three-time U.S. Open champion (1974, 1979, 1990) Hale Irwin, 58, has always reserved his most impressive performances for the most formidable courses, blending a precise iron game with a powerful will. Irwin, an outstanding defensive back at the University of Colorado in the mid-1960s, had 20 victories on the PGA Tour and has followed with a record 38 triumphs on the Champions Tour.

FIRST AND GOALS: "The discipline I maintained to play college football helped me through my early years, learning how to play and not giving up. I liked the contact, although I didn't like getting run over. I liked the camaraderie, the team aspect, and made some great friendships not only with my team members but with other players. At Winged Foot, we were all overwhelmed with the golf course, but I always felt a little overwhelmed on the football field, so that wasn't a strange position."

AN ENCORE AT AGE 45: "Winning the 1990 Open meant a great deal. I had devoted a number of years and certainly a lot of mental time to my design business. My thought process was geared more to that than it was to playing. After a period of nearly four years of really ragged play, I devoted the latter half of 1989 and the first part of 1990 to get myself back into playing form mentally. I did, and that's why it wasn't such a terrible surprise to me."

YOUNG AT HEART: "I have always loved competition, whether it be Little League baseball or sandlot basketball. The competition part keeps me young in feeling. If there comes a time where it looks like the best I can do is a 72 or a 73, I'm going to think very seriously about getting out and doing something else."

The final drive at the 1969 Open Championship at Royal Lytham St. Annes was probably my greatest shot.

I came to the 72nd hole with a two shot lead over Bob Charles and the knowledge that in past championships at Royal Lytham both Christy O'Connor of Ireland and Eric Brown of Scotland had needed par 4's to win and made 6's because they got tangled up in the deep bunkers on this very narrow driving hole.

I remember Bob Charles having the honour and hitting his drive just in to the right rough, he said he thought it had gone into a bunker. Fortunately for me I watched it finish and knew it was safe.

I felt a lot of pressure at that moment, but when the time came to start the back swing, I kept telling myself that this is what all the hard work was about, swing wide and smooth. As I was saying it I was doing it, completely in the moment.

Henry Longhurst's commentary probably said it best   "It was a corker" that split the middle of the fairway, which enabled me to go on to a 2 stroke victory.

Tony Jacklin

England's Tony Jacklin captured only four PGA Tour events, but two of them were major championships—the 1969 British Open and the 1970 U.S. Open. In 1985, Jacklin led the European team to its first Ryder Cup victory since 1957. Two years later, at Muirfield Village in Ohio, he was the captain again when the Europeans won the Cup for the first time on American soil. In 2002, Jacklin, 59, was inducted into the World Golf Hall of Fame.

THE CONCESSION: "[Jack Nicklaus conceding a match-halving putt to him in the 1969 Ryder Cup singles] was a wonderful thing to do and the right thing to do. I was with Jack a month ago at Royal St. George's. We were doing a golf day there for the Royal Bank of Scotland, and it came up in the question-and-answer period afterwards. We went through the whole thing again, Jack saying I would never have missed it. When asked how far it was, he said it was between 20 and 24 inches. It wasn't bloody four feet like some people say. I wrote a letter to him afterwards [in 1969], saying your gesture was something I'll always remember."

CAPTAIN TONY: "The highlight, of course, was the first Ryder Cup victory in America. Everybody points to 1985 as being a milestone, when we won the first time in 28 years, but for me, there's only one first, and that was the win in America. That was extraordinarily special and always will be. Firsts are important."

ONE REGRET: "Not moving to America after I won my two majors. Instead, I waited till the early 1990s, and here we shall stay. During my prime, I was busy all the time trying to keep the British public and the British media happy, and I got fed up with it. Had I been over here, the focus wouldn't have been on me. I needed to make America my main tour because that's where the best players were. That's where they always were. That's where they are now."

 Peter Jacobsen Productions, Inc.

May 9, 2001

Dear Ron:

The greatest shot I ever hit was in the final round of the PGA TOUR Qualifying School in 1976 in Brownsville, Texas. I needed a par four in the final hole of the "marathon" event to secure my TOUR card.

I hit my tee shot into the right side fairway bunker and was left with a 200 yard 4 iron to a green fronted by a water hazard. Plus, the wind and rain was playing tricks with our shots all day.

I am happy to report that I somehow got that 4 iron somewhere on the face of the club and got it on the green. Two putts later, and I was a member of the PGA TOUR. I still can't believe I got that shot on the green.

The greatest shot I ever saw was Bob <u>Gilder</u> double eagle 2 on the par 5, 18th hole at Westchester C.C. that helped him win the 1982 ? ? Tom Kite and I were paired with Bob in the 3rd round, chasing Bob for the title. Needless to say, from the middle of the fairway, Bob's 3 wood was perfect. It never left the flag. In fact, as it was in the air, I said out loud to my caddie Mike "Fluff" Cowan… "that's in!" I'll never forget that shot.

Best regards,

Peter Jacobsen

PJ/ml

Peter Jacobsen

In July 2003, Peter Jacobsen gave his supporters quite an encore with a most improbable second triumph at the Greater Hartford Open, 19 years after the first. Long recognized as one of the game's most colorful personalities, Jacobsen has posted seven victories in all, including two in a row during the tour's West coast swing in 1995. A three-time All-American from the University of Oregon, Jacobsen, 50, became eligible in 2004 for the Champions Tour.

LIGHTEN UP, GUYS: "If I shoot 70 and it takes four hours, I am probably spending a minute and a half or two minutes over the shots. I've got 240 minutes out there on the course. There's an opportunity to bond with the crowd, to bond with the earth, to talk to your playing partners. We get a little too much of the head down, behind-the-sunglasses, looking at our shoes, contemplating the pattern of divots underneath our feet. Thank God that the players in the game are like the ocean's tide, which ebbs and flows. We go from entertainers to serious players, back to entertainers, back to serious players, and it's been that way throughout the history of golf. We're ready to get back to some entertainers."

I GET S-A-T-I-S-F-A-C-T-I-O-N: "I felt like I got as much out of my career, if not more, than a lot of players did. Take the players who have more wins on tour than I do. Have they really been able to experience a lot of the things that I have done? I've done television. I've been in movies. I've written a book. I've done a CD. I've squeezed as much blood out of the turnip as I can."

I REMEMBER PAYNE STEWART: "When I beat him in a playoff at the Colonial in 1984, he shook my hand, gave me a hug, and said, 'Say hi to your dad for me.' My dad was in the hospital, having just had cancer surgery. I thought that was a lot of humility and class; he was thinking of me and not himself."

BETTY JAMESON
LPGA HALL OF FAME

7/17/03

Dear Ron,

Thanks for thinking of me. I am so thrilled to be included with my friends and the other great golfers of our time. It's been 71 years since I won the Texas State Public Championship at the age of 13 at the Wichita Falls, Texas municipal course where Bill Shawn was the professional. I have seen many wonderful shots and played with the greats of the game such as Bobby Jones and Babe Zaharias. Ben and Valerie Hogan took me under their wing and really treated me nice when I was getting started. Ben suggested I keep my right thumb and forefinger in a certain place over the left hand to keep the hands together. He showed me that the one time he played George May's Tam O'Shanter. Ben never played it again as George wanted the players to wear numbers on their backs and Ben didn't want to. Another thrill I had was knowing Francis Ouimet was in the gallery when I won the 1940 US Amateur at The Country Club in Brookline, Massachusetts.

On to my greatest shot. I was playing with Jo Ann Prentice at the first Virginia Hot Springs Four Ball in 1955 when we were both about 160 yards out. Jo Anne hit a great shot to about 5 feet, right on line with the stick. I asked her to please mark the ball. She was incredulous. She stomped her club several times as she marched down the fairway saying " Betty, you've got to be kidding!!!". I managed to hit it right on line inside her ball to about 3 feet. The funny thing is next week, Clifford Ann Creed asked me to do the same thing from slightly closer in.

A funny experience I would like to share with you was when I was playing with Jackie Pung. She was the player who did the hula when she won the US Open because she was from Hawaii. It was such a beautiful dance. One time, she got to the green on an uphill hole and was huffing and puffing. I had to ask her to "stop breathing, please!" before I putted. We all got a good laugh out of that.

The two tips I always share with players is to "take dead aim", which Harvey Penick taught me and my other tip was from Tommy Armour who said you swing like you waggle and to "hit the hell out of the ball with the right hand".

I've really enjoyed our conversations and hope to meet you sometime.

Sincerely,

Betty Jameson

Tournament Victories
Texas Publinx 1932, US Women's Amateur 1939 and 1940, Western Amateur and Western Open 1942, US Women's Open 1947, Tampa Open 1948, Texas Open 1949, Corpus Christi, Bakersfield Open (tied with Marlene Hagge, Betsy Rawls and Babe Zaharias), World Championship 1952, Servin Miami Beach Open 1953, Womens's Western Open 1954, Sarasota Open, Babe Zaharias Open, White Mountains Open, Richmond Open 1955

Betty Jameson

Betty Jameson, one of the LPGA's 13 founders, was the U.S. Women's Open champion in 1947 at Starmount Forest Country Club in Greensboro, North Carolina. She finished with a score of 295, the first time a female professional golfer shot lower than 300 in a 72-hole tournament. Jameson, 84, also has a pair of U.S. Women's Amateur titles (1939, 1940).

SHOW HER THE MONEY: "I thought I would never turn professional. I had no interest in being a pro, and was working at the *San Antonio Light* [the local newspaper]. I always wanted to be a writer. It didn't come to me easily, but I still love the written word. I got to be on the city desk, of all things, and covered Rotarian speeches. Spalding wanted somebody to put up against Wilson, which had gotten Patty Berg before the war. Patty and I were the two leading women golfers. They offered me $5,000 or $7,500 for the whole year."

LONG BEFORE ANNIKA: "I went to England with Babe in 1950. There were six of us. We went to play the women at Sunningdale. We were having a dinner party, and the men said, 'Let us play the girls.' Leonard Crawley was the guy who had the idea. He had a red mustache. So we played at Wentworth, foursomes in the morning and singles in the afternoon. On the night we were getting this all together, Babe, who was to play Crawley, said, 'I'll play you for your mustache.' She beat him. He got away without shaving it off. The conditions were dry, which is why we won. The men hit the ball higher and didn't get as much roll."

THE GLAMOUR GIRL: "I always liked to have the right thing on when I played golf. Glenna was my idol. [Glenna Collett Vare was a six-time U.S. Amateur champion in the 1920s and '30s.] She just had a certain poise about her. I always wore a string of pearls and I couldn't imagine playing golf in anything but a skirt."

Lee Janzen

With two U.S. Open titles on his resume, Lee Janzen, 39, belongs to a very select group. On both occasions, 1993 at Baltusrol Golf Club in New Jersey and 1998 at The Olympic Club in San Francisco, Janzen beat the late Payne Stewart down the stretch. A two-time Ryder Cup participant (1993, 1997), Janzen has won eight tournaments, including the 1995 Players Championship, the unofficial fifth major.

THE O'S: "We moved to Maryland when I was six years old. The stars were Brooks Robinson, Mark Belanger, Boog Powell, and they had four starters who all won 20 games. I remember watching Robinson gobble everything up in the 1970 World Series, beating the Reds in four straight. I've been to Camden Yards about 20 times. I got to meet Cal Ripken a few years ago when he was rehabbing his back. Sometimes we can't play when we have an ache or a pain, but when you do play, you have to put that aside and do your best."

TONY ROBBINS: "I learned some really good lessons from his stuff. I went over my notes again in April, and it just tightens your focus. You write down on paper as many reasons as you can why you want to accomplish [a certain goal] and what you're going to do with it. A lot of people are afraid of accomplishing big things. They hold themselves back. Overcoming fear is a huge step. As far as gifted athletic ability, the best to the least on the tour is probably not a huge difference. Mentally is where it's all made."

TAMING THE TEMPER: "I still may say something on the course I wish I hadn't said, but in no way does it compare to the way I acted when I was a junior golfer or in high school or in college or on the mini-tours . . . or even when I got on the tour. With cussing or slamming clubs, I just finally realized how I looked. It wasn't a very good example. There were times I fired myself up by doing it. I think I can fire myself up without showing my temper."

Lee Janzen

How do I decide what the greatest shot I have hit up to now is? There are many factors. The weather, course, tournament, pressure, difficulty of shot, or the most perfectly struck. I decided on a combination of all these factors.

The situation was the 1998 US Open during the final round on the 17th hole. I had played great from the fourth hole thru the 16th. At one time I was 7 shots behind Payne Stewart, the leader, and I was now tied for the lead. I hit a perfect drive on one of the toughest driving holes in golf. This was the third day in a row that I hit perfect drives. The prior two days resulted in double bogeys.

For the week I had played the 17th hole five over par. This hole could easily cost me the tournament. On Saturday I had 221 yards to the hole. The pin was in the back and I was in a divot that had almost grown back in. I hit it great with a 3 iron, but the ball landed in the middle of the green and bounced over leading to a six.

(1)

Lee Janzen

On Sunday the hole was cut on the front right of the green. My yardage from the fairway was about 215 yards. This is about how far I flew my 3 iron on Saturday. I figured the same shot would be the right distance. The front of the green is very narrow making the target a lot smaller. The fairway also slopes left to right severely. The wind was blow left to right and slightly in. The temperature was in the mid 60s.

With the US Open on the line and all the other factors I figured I would have to hit my best 3 iron with a slight fade. I hit my shot as solid as I could with a slight fade. The ball landed near the front of the green on a downslope of the front right bunker. The ball bounced to the back of the green. I made a great a 2-putt for par and went on to win my second U.S. Open.

So the pressure, lie, shot, past rounds, and weather played a factor in this shot that I have chosen. A 3 iron second shot on the 71ST hole of the 1998 U.S. Open.

(2)

Steve Jones

The year was 1988. The tournament was the AT&T Pebble Beach National Pro-Am.

I was faced with a 145 yd. uphill second shot, on the par 4 18th hole at Cypress Point Golf Club. The green is severely sloped from back to front. ~~I as seven~~ I hit a seven iron 30 Ft. over the pin knowing it would come back to the hole.

My wife Bonnie was coming out of the club house at the moment my shot landed, she asked "who's ball is that?" "Jones", said the gallery.

They all watched the ball spin back perfectly into the hole for a 64. I went on to win my first PGA Tour Event.

Cypress was and still is my most favorite course in the world.

Steve Jones

In June 1996, Steve Jones turned in the performance of his career, edging Tom Lehman on the 72nd hole of the U.S. Open at Oakland Hills. The victory climaxed a remarkable comeback for Jones, who missed nearly three years after seriously injuring his ring finger in a 1991 dirt-bike accident. Jones, 45, has won eight tournaments, including three in 1989 when he finished eighth on the money list.

MAGIC, MAYHEM: "Everything at Oakland Hills went right as far as the golf. Everything went wrong outside the golf course. We got to this guy's house on Sunday, but the keys weren't under the mat, so we had to break into a window so we could sleep there that night. They had water, but their well was polluted, so we couldn't use it. The TV had two stations. It was one thing after another. But I got to the course and felt great, and practice was really good. Reading the book on Ben Hogan helped: Give all your effort to each shot and don't worry about the outcome. I did that pretty much every shot and stayed in the moment."

LIKE CLOCKWORK: "It seems like every ten years, something happens to me. In 1981, I broke my thumb and took a year off. In 1991, I had the motorcycle wreck. Last year, I started having elbow problems. But I won four tournaments after the injuries in 1991. Sometimes you need that motivation. It kind of extended my career a little bit. After eight years in a row of playing, you start to get burned out a little bit. Before my game gets too terrible, I have an injury, and it kind of revives me when I come back, making me hungry to play."

THANKS, GUYS: "Hal Sutton helped me on my follow-through in 1989, keeping my left knee straight after impact. Dale Douglass helped me with my sand play. I worked on those tips and used them, and went to the first tournament, not expecting much. Boom, I won La Costa and then I won Bob Hope the following week."

The shot that gets number one status was a pure shot, but has two parts which gives it the rating. Actually, three parts, the first being the setting—the 1995 U.S. Open at Shinnecock in Long Island. There is no finer setting in golf.

Part two was the shot, Friday afternoon on cut day, and I was on the edge. I needed a couple of birdies and would make my first Open cut. Being from New England and having lived in New Jersey, I had a very large gallery of friends and family.

It's the fourteenth hole, and I have 192 yards to the stick. I'm pumped up and have the perfect club, six iron. As I made contact, I knew that I'd flushed it. Artie, my longtime friend and looper, and a resident of South Hampton, called out his usual "be the schtick." It was the "schtick," and rolled dead perfect in the cup.

Part three comes as me and Artie are running down the slopes "high-fiving" everyone, a la Hale Irwin. It was a crosswalk and Scottie Peters had crossed before the shot, so I had to cross the fairway, too, and ham it up with my dear friend. Just before I reached him, wading through knee-high fescue, I looked down and found a wad of hundred-dollar bills!

Scott was as stunned as I was, and, since it was in knee-deep rough, I assumed it was Seve's and stuck it in my pocket. We toasted Seve that night at the local tavern, not only for being my longtime hero and idol, but also for buying the drinks!

Jeff Julian

In the fall of 2001, Jeff Julian was diagnosed with ALS, known more commonly as Lou Gehrig's disease. With help from his wife, Kimberly, he has displayed tremendous courage, setting up a foundation to raise money for research. Julian, 42, was an assistant professional at the Quechee Club in Vermont before qualifying for the PGA Tour in 1996.

HOOKED ON GOLF: "As I grew up, my father would take me to Hanover Country Club for his weekend golf games. I was happy to go for two reasons: I got to drive the cart occasionally, and escaped a house full of five sisters, three of them teenagers. Every time we got to #17, a downhill par three, Dad would let me try a shot at the green. That became my reason for going to the course. I looked forward to that shot all morning! It started out as a three-wood dribbled off the end of the tee box, and then became a three-wood almost to the green. The next summer, it was a five-wood, then a four-iron. By the time I was twelve or thirteen, I was hooked on the feel of the ball hitting the sweet spot."

PEBBLE: "I have such great memories of that week [at the Pebble Beach National Pro-Am in February 2002]. Missing the cut was memorable, but not in the usual way. It left Sunday open for a round at Cypress with my playing partner, Pard Erdman, and our fellow competitor for the week, Don Beall. Kimberly, Betsy Erdman, and two of my sisters joined us for what is the most beautiful walk in golf. The pictures of that day hang on our living room wall."

NO SURRENDER: "It's easy to explain what I've learned from having to deal with ALS. Simply, I am not alone. Kimberly, I already knew, is an amazing woman. Our families have been tremendous support, and that is no surprise. The tour and everyone involved made it very clear that we are a part of the family, and that has been a great comfort. What has surprised me the most is the depth of friendship people have afforded us. Our closest friends have given time and effort to be sure we have everything we need to fight our battle."

Jerry Kelly

After six solid seasons on the PGA Tour, Jerry Kelly, 37, finally broke through in 2002, winning the Sony Open in Hawaii and the Western Open outside Chicago, and finished sixth on the money list with nearly $3 million. He recorded eight Top 10s in 29 starts. Growing up in Wisconsin, Kelly fell in love with the Green Bay Packers and ice hockey.

THE PACK IS MOST DEFINITELY BACK: "We went through a lot of lean years. Every single year was going to be the turnaround year. You would get so excited and then you would end up getting crushed. Once Brett Favre got there, everything changed. Favre just put the team on his shoulders. It was pretty incredible. Finally, when they won, I got to say something to all the players out here. I was being kicked for way too long."

ON THIN ICE: "I usually wasn't one of the best on the team. I was very fast and I could score and I could pass, but I didn't have the vision for hockey. I skated so hard, I probably skated with my head down with the puck too much. A lot of players skate with their head up. The puck sticks to their stick and they can just see one step ahead and anticipate. They know what they're going to do and they can sense what the defenseman is going to do."

PRIME TIME: "Everything is coming together. I feel like my best golf is in front of me. I've still got work to do on my swing and putting, and my mental game has farther to go than I would like. I'm a perfectionist. A lot of people, when they visualize their round beforehand, they have a hard time seeing themselves hit perfect golf shots. When I visualize a round before I play, I shoot 52, 53, 54. I have a hard time making myself putt because I make the iron shot. I make twos on par fives. That kind of perfection in my mind doesn't translate well to patience and acceptance on a golf course."

JERRY KELLY

My greatest shot may be just a regular little eight-iron shot to many people. But the circumstances and the mental impact it had on me made this shot the one.

At the 2002 Western Open I was a local favorite. As many tickets as I could find went to family and friends. Not many tournaments do I get calls from the gallery like Tiger gets every week. Winning the first tournament of the year put more pressure on me to perform in front of the "hometown" fans. I had played well for the year but wondered if the first win come on a "soft" week. A good field but was everyone just rusty on the first week. Not great thoughts to have after finally winning your first PGA Tour event after 200 starts.

JERRY KELLY

I had just birdied the 11th and 12th holes for a one shot lead. Now facing one of the toughest holes on the back side. I overswung on the 480-yard into-the-wind hole pulling the ball well left into a fairway bunker. There was a tree dead in front of me ten yards away. All I could do was wedge the ball to the fairway. Now I have left myself 148 yards to a pin tucked four yards from the front of the green and three yards from the left edge. There is a 15 foot slope guarding the front of the green. The wind was in my face. Knowing I hit my eight iron 150 yards and the shot playing about 158 yards, eight iron was the only club to hit the ball close. The seven hit easy would not hold enough spin to keep it close.

JERRY KELLY

Anything short of a perfect hard draw with the eight would end up in the bank in deep rough. As I hit the shot my caddy said "get up!", I calmly said to him "no, it's perfect". The ball landed on the fringe and hopped up to within four feet. I made the par putt and looked up at the next tee which overlooks the green. Davis Love's caddy Cubby looked at me smiled and shook his head. At that point I knew I wasn't going to back up. I could get through any bad shot, even when in the lead. I proceeded to birdie the next two holes on my way to a two shot win. All thanks to purely struck hard eight iron under pressure.

Christina Kim

Dear Michael,

You first came up to me in April, telling me about a book you were putting together. A book about the greatest shots hit by some of the world's best golfers. I thought it was a neat idea, and wished I could be a part of that book. Yet when you asked me to think of the greatest shot I had hit and send it to you in a letter, I was terrified. I have spent the last several months agonizing over the greatest shot I have ever hit, when it hit me. The greatest shot that I had ever hit was what many would consider one of the easiest shots in golf, and that may be the case. For me, however, there was much more than just the shot that made it my greatest.

I was playing in the final round of the Garden State Hewlett-Packard Futures Classic in Manalapan, New Jersey, and I was duking it out with Lorena Ochoa. At the end of regulation, we were both 14-under, and off we went in a sudden-death playoff. We both parred our first five holes uneventfully in the 104 degree heat, and coming down the seventeenth hole, our sixth hole, I told myself, this is it. I don't know who is going to win, but I know that this is our last hole. We both hit our teeshots on the 340-yard par 4, and walking up to our shots, a sudden sense of calm came over me. I walked to the green, measured the shot at 62 yards, pulled out my lob wedge, and swung away. It sailed high and made a beeline for the flag, which perched close to the back edge of the elevated green. I could not tell where exactly the ball was, but I knew it was close. There was a lot of applause, and when I got to the green, there my ball lay, seven inches from the cup. After Lorena missed her putt for birdie (by like, an inch, I must add) I calmly tapped mine in for my very first professional win.

All of those months, those years of hard work finally paid off. I had spent so much time putting in my heart, soul, my very essence to become the best player I could be. I knew that I could win in my heart, but my mind had begun to waver. I had been runner-up three times before, having been so close to winning, and when I finally broke through, the dark clouds finally parted. That shot proved to me that I did have the ability to win against the pros.

I turned professional on my 18th birthday, and many people did not think that I made the right choice in passing college to play at the professional level, but with that win, leading me to finish the season second on the money list and earning my LPGA Tour exempt status for 2003, I proved to those nay-sayers that I belong here with the world's best. I hope that this letter finds you well, and that this letter makes the cut for your book.

Love, Peace, and Birdies through life,

Christina Kim, 2003 LPGA Tour Rookie

Christina Kim

The affable Christina Kim, 20, compiled a more than respectable rookie season in 2003, finishing 49th on the money list with two Top 10 finishes. Kim, who received an automatic promotion to the LPGA Tour by finishing second in earnings on the Futures Tour, holds the record for the lowest 18-hole score in a USGA event, firing an eight-under 62 in the 2001 U.S. Girls' Junior Championship.

SORENSTAM SIGHTING: "Tuesdays are the official practice day. The Tuesday at the Office Depot tournament in Los Angeles was on April Fool's Day. I played one round early in the morning and signed up to play another round in the afternoon. I put my name down, Kim C, for 1:37. After lunch, when I went back to look to make sure I had 1:37 and not 1:25, I saw there were two names next to mine. One said Sorenstam, and I thought, Wow, Charlotta, that's neat. But the other name was also Sorenstam. I thought that is so mean. Someone was playing a really nasty April Fool's joke on me. I walked to the tee box, and they both were there, Annika and Charlotta. I was awestruck. I spent a good part of the day picking Annika's brain."

GOING LOW: "I was just on auto pilot. No matter what I did [during the round of 62], all my putts went in. There was nothing I could do about it. I think I missed one fairway and I know I missed only one green. I was hitting irons really tight, attacking everything. I was playing smart and aggressive."

THANKS, DAD: "My dad introduced me to golf. I knew about the game because my parents played for a couple of years, but I was focusing so much on school at the time. For the first couple of months, I swung the club 500 times a day without ever hitting a ball. I got used to the motion of the swing. Eventually, I went to the range and started hitting balls. If it hadn't been for my father, I wouldn't be where I am."

The Greatest Shot I Ever Hit
By Robert Landers

There are four or five shots that come to mind. Almost all of them were more the result of good luck rather than one of those desperate shots that actually worked out exactly like planned. This shot happened at a Nitro Senior Series event in Evansville, Indiana. The year was 1997. The tournament was at Rolling Hills Country Club, a course that had five or six par fours with second shots that were extremely uphill.

I played a very steady tournament that week and found myself starting out the final round tied for the lead after rounds of 66 and 69. This was the first time I had ever been close to the final group in the last round.

On the last day, I found myself standing on the eighteenth tee one shot behind Dick Ryan and two ahead of Chuck Thorpe at ten under par. This hole was 520-yard par five that had a big trap on the left and a tree lined right side of the fairway. The tee shot was a bit up hill with an impossible lay-up to a very steep down slope all the way to the water. There was only about 20 yards from the one hundred-yard marker to the water and there was something like thirty-five yards on the other side in front of the green. I hit a very big fade (slice) that went deep into the trees. Dick Ryan hit a perfect shot and was standing on the two hundred marker. I found my ball in a worn area where at address, I was standing on a cart path and was entitled to a free drop. I had to drop on hard pan and was very lucky that it didn't roll when dropped. I told my wife Freddie "that this was going to be do or die." For sure, Dick had a four iron to the middle of the green. If I hit it in the water, I could still make 6 and tie Chuck for second. I had never had a chance to win before so if I could pull this off, I would have a chance to tie Dick if he made par and I made birdie. I pulled out my 15 degree Goldwin three wood and accessed the shot. In my backswing, there was a tree that my clubhead missed by only an inch. I was 235 to the front of the green and I had to go under a bushy topped tree forty yards ahead of my ball with a slight cut. I hit the shot the shot almost exactly as planned. It stopped in heavy rough just short of the green where I hit a flop lob wedge 2 feet from the hole to make birdie. Dick pulled his second shot left of the green where he couldn't get up and down for birdie.

We went back to the 18th tee. Both tee shots were right down the middle. I was standing on the 200 yard marker and Dick was at 205. He hit first and pulled it almost in the same spot where he was a few minutes earlier. I had a 4 iron out and after seeing Dick's shot, I immediately told Freddie to give me a 5 iron. I ain't gonna hit this ball past the pin, no way. I hit the 5 almost exactly where I had birdied a few moments earlier. It was impossible with the ball sitting down in thick rough and very little green to work with. Dick hit his chip 25 feet from the hole and then two putted. My lob landed softly and stopped 18 inches from the cup. This was the biggest win of my life and still is today. The three wood and two lob shots are something I'll never forget. It was my first win since turning pro and it was against two players who played on the Senior Tour.

Robert Landers

The Champions Tour, the most successful mulligan in professional sports, has produced its share of surprises, none more unlikely than the remarkable rise of Texas farmer Robert Landers. In 1994, Landers qualified for the tour, going right into battle against the game's legends. He competed for a couple of years, becoming an inspiration to middle-aged dreamers everywhere. Landers, 60, has returned to the farm.

NINE TO EIGHT: "I started at Mitchell's Department Store when I was a junior in high school. I worked through school until I went into the military, and then spent two years in the insurance business. I went back to Mitchell's in 1972 and worked there till 1992, when the company went out of business. I was a store manager. Our hours were 9 in the morning till 8 in the evening. I could never get off two days in a row, and that was one of the things that kept me from playing much golf. I'm not an inside guy, and I was stuck in that job. I would still be there, probably, if they were still open."

PAUL BUNYAN, NOT RUNYAN: "We raise beef cattle, raising hay to feed the cattle. We have about 200 acres that we're looking after. The main thing is that every time there's a storm, there are gates you have to shut and fences you have to check to see if any trees fell on them. There is no milking of cows, just a beef deal. One of the things I do in the wintertime is that I cut and sell a little bit of firewood. The physical activity keeps me going."

HIS 15 MINUTES: "It was two years, a long time ago, and it was quite a whirlwind. The favorite thing I had about it was knowing the accomplishment. I never dreamed it. It was out of reach for an average person. I had spent most of my life trying to promote golf in the community. My only dream was to simply have a golf course built in Azle, Texas, and by doing so, that's how I got on tour, by practicing."

Thomas Levet

Dear Michael

If I have one shot to tell about, it would be the putt I made to win the tournament in Cannes in 1998 on the European Tour. I was not exempt after a miserable 1996 and a frustrating year on the Challenge Tour. At this time, I was struggling big time money wise. Nobody makes a fortunate on the Challenge Tour. I was teaching a little bit in clubs around Paris to keep my family ok. At one stage, I had only 10 francs (less than two dollars) in my account, and this tournament, even if one of the smallest on tour, was one of only three chances to play for bigger money.

After two weeks of practice in freezing Paris, where I was shooting low scores every day and beating all my friends, I came to Cannes with a special feeling, very confident for an underdog who never won anything outside the French Tour. After Tuesday practice, where my pro colleagues were impressed with my game, I even told one of them, "If I keep playing on like that, I'm gonna win this thing," (keep on dreaming, he must have thought).

Going into the last day, I was, in fact, leading by four over tour veteran Eammon Darcy. I had never been in the lead before on the European Tour, so I was a bit anxious. On the fourth day, the weather turned to really ugly, and like every other player, I dropped shot after shot. But I stood on the last hole, a par 5, needing only a six to win. There was water everywhere.

After a good drive that finished just inches in the rough, I can't hit the green that is only 220 yards away, so I decide to lay up past the bunkers on the fairway. My ball is well over my feet. I hit this shot a bit high on the club's face, and it finishes in the worst bunker on the fairway. I hit a shot from 100 yards with a sand wedge that hit the lip of the bunker and plugs in the trap again. So now I have only three shots left to win, and it doesn't look good. The water is not in play anymore, but the green is maybe the toughest I know in the world.

I manage to put my 8 iron on the green, sixty feet from the hole, but with a plateau to go through sideways. If I hit it right, it goes in the bunker. If I hit it too much left, it is possible that I go down the slope and finish 120 feet from the hole. It finished about eight feet from the hole, and then I was facing THE PUTT. If it goes in, I win, and go back on the main tour, I win a bit of money, probably get new sponsors, and life is suddenly better. If it doesn't, I'm in a playoff with three other guys. Second is not good enough.

As I stood over it, I remembered the words of Eduardo Romero, who once said about a similar situation: 'Don't worry if it doesn't go in, you still have a chance.' This made me immediately calmer. I putted it just like I was on the putting green, and, to this day, I still remember the feeling of it. I used a bullseye putter, and even if I don't play with it anymore, I sometimes go to see "him" in my garage just for the souvenir of it.

Thomas Levet

France's Thomas Levet spent most of his career in Europe before taking on the PGA Tour in 2003. Levet, a two-time winner on the European Tour, nearly recorded the biggest victory of his life in the 2002 British Open at Muirfield, falling in a sudden-death playoff to Ernie Els. Levet showed wonderful sportsmanship, lifting the six-foot-three Els off the ground. In the early 1980s, Levet, 35, was a nationally ranked tennis player.

MAKING A NAME: "A lot more people after the Open began to focus on what I was doing, especially in my country, all because I played good in that one tournament and put my world ranking a little bit higher. People know my face and my name at the moment, when before, they knew my name and my face but not together. You wish that someday you'll be fighting for the win in a major tournament, and when it happens, it's unreal. Was I disappointed to finish second? A little bit, of course, but if you don't enjoy finishing second in a major tournament, you'll never enjoy anything. There are worse things that can happen."

A BOY OF ALL SPORTS: "I played field hockey quite a lot, and I played tennis six times a week for three hours a day. But I picked up golf because it was the one I liked the most. The atmosphere was better than the atmosphere at tennis tournaments. People in tennis take it very seriously at a very young age. When you're 13 years old and you see two guys fighting because the ball was an inch out or an inch in, you wonder, is this a sport or is this a fight?"

THERE'S NO PLACE LIKE HOME: "I miss the food in France, and I miss seeing my friends on the European Tour. Here, there is no change in food from one city to the other, no different cultures. You don't go from Sweden to Italy or from Scotland to Spain. In Europe, I was an hour or two hours, max, away from home. I could go home every Sunday, and even practice there on Monday and Tuesday."

Hilary Lunke

Only the most devoted LPGA fans recognized the name of Hilary Lunke when it popped up on the leaderboard during last summer's U.S. Women's Open at Pumpkin Ridge. With a birdie on the final hole of an 18-hole playoff, Lunke prevailed over Angela Stanford and Kelly Robbins for her first tournament victory. Lunke, 24, was a four-time All-American at Stanford and played in seven U.S. Women Amateurs.

SINK OR SWIM: "Golf and swimming were the same season in high school. I decided that even if it didn't work out for golf, I thought I could play it for the rest of my life. Swimming may have ended up being a ticket to college, but in the long run, it wasn't something I wanted to be doing. Swimming is one of the most incredibly disciplined sports. If you skipped a practice session, you could feel it the next workout. You had to be extremely disciplined with your physical training. It's helped me with golf mentally."

LEARNING HOW TO SCORE: "I played on the boys' golf team my sophomore year in high school. It was extremely difficult because our home golf course was over 7,000 yards long. This was six years ago, when most golf courses weren't 7,000 yards. There were a lot of huge carries off the tee. It was hard for me to even break 90. I couldn't get near the green to try to get up and down. Maybe that's how I learned to score. I learned creative ways to make pars, to make bogeys when you should be making doubles."

THE SHORT ANSWER: "There is no doubt that I wish I hit the ball farther, but, at the same time, I take pride in the fact that I can shoot the scores that I do with as short as I hit it. I have a great short game and hit the ball straight. If I could get longer distance, I would be a much better player, but I'm not going to sacrifice the assets I have as a player in order to get that distance."

9/25/03

Dear Ron...

Sorry its taken me a little
bit to write you... best of luck with your book! Hope this entry
helps...

    Many people may think that the obvious choice for the best shot
I've ever hit would be the 15 ft. putt that I made in a playoff to
win the 2003 U.S. Open, but the truth is, my greatest shot came
the day before. After two poor shots at the 72nd hole of the
Championship, I faced a 110 yard fairway bunker shot. I had a
good lie in the sand, but I needed to hit it high enough to clear
the lip, hit it low enough to stay under some overhanging trees,
and I had about only 6 feet of room left or right of the pin to keep the
ball on the green! I'm not the greatest out of fairway bunkers either, ⟶

So this was not the shot I wanted to have to execute. I backed off the shot once and said a silent prayer: "Lord, I cannot pull this shot off on my own, you're going to have to do it for me." And right then and there I hit the greatest shot of my life considering the circumstances: the ball flew out perfectly, landed a few paces on the green, and ended up about 18 ft. short of the flagstick, allowing me to easily make par and earn a spot in the playoff which I would go on to win the next day.

Meg Mallon

Since the early 1990s, Meg Mallon has been one of the most consistent performers on the LPGA Tour, winning 15 tournaments, including three major championships. In 1991, she captured the U.S. Women's Open, the LPGA Championship, and recorded 12 Top 10s in 26 starts. Mallon, 41, has made seven appearances in the Solheim Cup.

EVERGREEN: "The 1963 Boston Celtics were at my christening in our house in South Natick, Massachusetts, and they have been friends of the family ever since. My father worked for the Ford Motor Company, and the Celtics did some promotional work for Ford. Somehow, he was involved in that and got to know them. Even after we moved to Detroit, we saw them when they played the Pistons and maintained the friendships with Tom Heinsohn, Bob Cousy, and K. C. Jones. I remember my dad pacing around the house [during the NBA playoffs]; I believe I saw my dad cry for the first time when they won."

BUCKING THE STATE: "I was booed on either side of the border, for going to Ohio State and being from Michigan. It took me till my junior year to actually cheer for the Ohio State football program because I was such a Michigan fan. Now I cheer for Michigan . . . except when they play Ohio State. I was actually offered a scholarship at Michigan State. While I was on my recruiting trip, the Michigan State coach said, 'Well, Ohio State is the best team in the Big 10, but with your help, we can come close to them.' I sent a letter to Ohio State. They didn't have any scholarships, but the program was so fantastic."

LIFE BEGINS AT 40: "I don't know why they put women out to pasture younger than men. The men are playing into their 50s and 60s. After we turn 40, it seems like our games should fall apart. But, if anything, some players have gotten better. Look at Juli Inkster. She's won 15 times since 1997, since she turned 37 years old. It's a game for the ages."

Meg Mallon

1991 LPGA Championship~

Pat Bradley, Ayako Okamoto and
myself were tied on the 72nd
Tee box. I teed off last and a
car on the road right behind the
tee blew its horn on my backswing. I
flinched but still hit it in the
fairway. I was a good 30 yards behind
my opponents in the fairway. The pin
was tucked in the back left corner of
the green and I chose a five iron to

try and get back of the green without going over. Under the circumstances I hit the best shot of my life the ball landed 10 feet to the left of the hole as though it were on a string from my club. My opponents had 8 and 9 irons in and had 20 and 30 footers for birdie, we all had a shot to win but I was fortunate enough to make the putt and win my first Major Championship. I'll never forget that moment ~ Thanks for allowing me to draw that wonderful memory up again ~ CPhg

Roger Maltbie

NBC on-course commentator Roger Maltbie came through with some of his best performances in the biggest events. In 1976, Maltbie prevailed in the first Memorial Tournament, defeating Hale Irwin in a playoff. Almost a decade later, he was triumphant at Westchester and Firestone, two of the tour's most challenging layouts, and finished eighth on the money list. Maltbie, 52, plays rarely on the Champions Tour.

A MAJOR OPPORTUNITY: "I had a shot at winning the Masters in 1987. I was in the last group with Crenshaw. At 18, I piped it into the center of the fairway. With the hole cut in the traditional front left, I was trying to use the slope in back of the hole. I couldn't have made a better swing. The ball should have hit that slope and come back down near the hole, at least giving me some putt to choke on. Instead, when there was no reaction from the crowd, I knew it had gotten up on the top, about 35 feet away. You know nobody ever made that putt."

MEETING MR. BRODIE: "At San Jose Country Club, where I was raised, they hosted the Santa Clara County Amateur Championship every year. One year, I got paired with John Brodie [the San Francisco 49ers' star quarterback]. I was probably 15 or so. I guess I was playing a golf ball that was less than ready for prime time. When we were done, he said, 'Come with me.' I followed him to his car. He opened his trunk and had a shoebox full of Titleists. 'You're too good to play with those old things,' he said."

NO MULLIGAN: "I've got young kids, 16 and 13. We started our family kind of late, and they need their dad to be home. Fortunately, I make a nice enough living so I don't have to worry about that. To go back out there full-time would be kind of a selfish exercise. I never dreamt about winning anything on the Senior Tour. If I was going to be the next Jack Nicklaus, I would have done that by now."

ROGER MALTBIE

Dear Michael,

"What was the best shot I ever hit?" That is a big question, Michael, and one that requires serious reflection. Like it or not, somehow…someway, the life of a professional golfer will be measured by the quality of the golf shots they have produced in competition. More specifically those played under pressure in the biggest of moments. In this instance you have asked about the best shot, the **ONE** that has mattered to me the most. Most people would think it would be a shot that was played under the glaring eye of national television, the shot that completed the big comeback or cemented the victory. I've been fortunate and have struck a few of those shots along the trail. Which shot mattered the most? Which shot had more meaning? Which shot did more to advance my professional career?

In my case it was a shot played with very few people as witnesses. There was no television, no public scrutiny, and no money on the line. No, this shot didn't mean much to anybody but me, my family, and my friends. It certainly wasn't majestic or brilliant. In fact, it really didn't take any talent at all. It was…**A CHIPOUT.**

In the fall of 1974 I attended the Qualifying School for the second time. It was the final round (the 144th hole) at Canyon Country Club in Palm Springs, California. That year the finals were contested over a two week period. They were two 72 hole events, so to speak. Thursday through Sunday of the first 72 were played at Silverado Country Club in Napa, California. After this we traveled to Palm Springs, practiced and prepared for the final 72 holes which were played Thursday through Sunday again.

Those of you unfamiliar with Q-school probably would not understand the pressure involved. It is the player's one chance annually to make it to the Tour. Make it to the big leagues, a shot at pursuing their life's dream, pretty big stuff. The pressure? Well, let's just say it's like playing the final hole of a tournament with the lead each and every hole. To top it all off there are no scoreboards for the players to view as they play the final holes in what surely is the biggest tournament of their lives.

I was very fortunate to have my lifelong friend, Frank Pieper, with me as my caddie these two weeks. Frank, as the son of former two-time California State Amateur Champion Ernie Pieper, Jr. and a fine player himself, was very experienced about the game and me as we had played golf together dating back to our pre-teen years. We had played high school golf together and Frank had just recently returned home from caddying for Forrest Fezler (another of my high school teammates) on the PGA Tour. He was just what I needed to help me get through the Q-school.

On that final Sunday I (was choking my guts out just like everyone else) found myself on the 18th hole believing I needed a birdie to qualify. The last hole at Canyon Country Club was a par five, dog leg left, and very reachable in two shots with OB left and water in play on the second shot. There was a lone date palm tree at the corner of the dog leg down the left hand side and I had played a little too aggressively from the tee with my ball coming to rest a couple of feet from the base of that tree. There was no obstacle in the flight path of my ball if I elected to go for the green with my second shot. The lie was perfect (there was no rough). There was no wind. The distance to the green was easily manageable. The only problem was that **Gxx dxxxxx** tree! By the time I reached my ball I had entered the final and most dangerous faze of choking...**I CAN DO THINGS NO MAN HAS EVER DONE!** I was going to hit a three wood, draw it ever so slightly, carry the water short of the green (about 220 yds.), make birdie and qualify for the PGA TOUR. Except...there was that x/?!X/] tree. No problem, I figured as I carefully and very slowly rehearsed my intended swing, after impact (let's say about 15 inches after) the middle of the club's shaft would contact the tree resulting in a clean break of the shaft. No problem I thought I can just pretend the tree isn't there and that it wouldn't affect my swing. This of course would leave me free to play the greatest shot ever struck by anyone ever...on this planet...or any other planet for that matter. I was ready!

My next course of action was to detail my brilliantly crafted and of course infallible plan to Frank. He laughed. I said, "I mean it". He laughed again. I insisted I could do this. He didn't laugh this time, he simply said no. Again, I assured him I could do it. Frank covered the clubs with the towel and his arms. "No way" he said. By now I really thought I was bullet proof...I continued to insist. This time he made it easier to understand. "I will kick your _xxx_ before I'll let you try that shot. Chip it out down the fairway, knock it on the green, make a putt...you qualify. Even if you make 5 you might still qualify". (Did I neglect to mention he was much bigger and stronger than I?) Forget about the battle over the 3 wood. I was going to get hammered! I changed my mind and complied with Frank's wish.

The result? I ended up birdieing the hole his way and qualified for the tour, avoided a trip to the emergency room, and enjoyed a life that could only be described as 'every golfer's dream. I can think of no other shot that has had as long and profound an effect on my career as that simple chip out in fall of 1974.

Sincerely,

Carol Mann

Carol Mann, 63, was a dominant player in the 1960s and '70s, winning 38 times and finishing in the Top 25 on the money list 16 straight years. Her victory total includes two majors: the 1964 Women's Western Open Invitational and the 1965 U.S. Women's Open. Mann, a member of the World Golf Hall of Fame, teaches at Woodlands Country Club in Texas and gives motivational speeches.

A DIFFERENT CROWD: "I played because of my dad. I wanted to spend time with him. The other appealing thing was that there were caddies who looked different than any people I had ever seen. They were poor and had funny clothes. One caddie, who befriended me for decades, had no front teeth. I had never seen anyone who had no front teeth. Golf was full of these interesting people and situations. Nobody I had ever seen looked or talked like these people. I had been in ballet studios and had taken piano lessons and went to a private girls school, wearing a uniform every day."

ROAD TRIP: "We caravanned in groups of four to eight cars, from tournament to tournament, on two-lane highways. If you were in the lead car, you had to stay out in the left-hand lane when you passed a truck, so everyone could get by. It was very dangerous. We would drive until the wee hours of the morning on difficult roads, starting Sunday night to get to the next place. We did laundry together, we shopped together. I shopped in a gang of eight. We did word games in the car. It was fun."

GOLF IN THE KINGDOM: "I believe in it. It's all very male, I know, but women can get it, too. If you're the least bit spiritual, and I don't mean religious, it's very appealing. Hundreds of thousands of people have played the game before us. The fact that the game is so old is an enchanting notion, that we're part of a legacy of all those people who started it and nurtured it and spread it, and loved it enough to do that."

Carol Mann

June 29, 2003

I was leading the 1965 US Open at Atlantic City Country Club going into the 16th hole of the final round by one shot. The 16th is a par four of 400 yards into a prevailing wind. A stream ran down the right side and crossed in front of the green about 70 yards out.

It was a fairly benign hole, until the eve-of-the-final-round anxiety took hold. I couldn't get to sleep, tossing and turning, wondering, winning and losing the Open about 40 times. Who knows why these things happen? When I finally fell asleep, I had a vivid nightmare. Upon reaching the tee at 16, I selected the driver and knocked the ball over the stream on the right, over the out of bounds fence and into the New Jersey marsh. Oh my gosh! I just lost the Open.

I woke up and immediately committed to a new game plan for 16. Only a three wood would see action for the first shot. All morning, waiting to tee off, I couldn't stop thinking about the first shot on that 16th. I had never experienced anything like this. I shook, felt nausea and got sweaty palms just with a mental glimpse of this hole. Was I going to allow myself to become powerless in the face of one shot? Was I this out of control? Was this normal when you lead the Open? Could I please skip that hole?

As the round progressed toward my fate, I accumulated pars but felt pressured to somehow get a birdie or two before I arrived, in case I needed a cushion. Easy and hard pars were all I could manage.

Several thousand people were watching at this point, including my parents and three of my four brothers, along with friends who had traveled up from my hometown of Baltimore. But none of them were aware of my nightmare.

I walked from the 15th green slowly toward the next tee. If only they knew. Maybe someone would help me, maybe they would call out, "You can do it!" I needed strength from somewhere to even take the club out of the b... Believe me, I did not want to play this shot. Unlike so many other sports, rules of this game don't allow time outs or substitutions. But I surely wa...ed both. At no time before or since for a total of my twenty-one year career have I faced demons like this.

Three wood ... thwop ... ball in the air ... headed right. Oh no! Wait ... it's not out. It landed three feet inside the fence on the bank of the stream, teetering on the edge of its own pit mark.

The ball was sitting so precariously that I could only choose a shot to lay up short of the stream in front of the green, then wedged on and sank a twenty footer for a crucial par. Then made par at 17 and birdie on the final hole to win the US Open Championship by two shots. I cried – mostly out of the incredible relief I felt that the hardest, toughest test in all of golf was over.

Best regards,

Carol Mann

Carol Mann

McCUMBERGOLF

When I look back over 25 years of professional golf on the PGA Tour it is hard to come up with one shot that stands out as my best, the greatest. My mind races to the seven foot putt I made on the last hole of Doral to win my first tournament in 1979, to the holing out of my last shot of the day from 117 yards in the first round of the 1988 Players Championship, to making a hole in one on the 10th hole at Winged Foot during the first round of the 1984 United States Open. And so many others….but narrowing it down to one, it would have to be "the putt" that won me the 1994 year-ending Tour Championship on the 18th at Olympic Club. Even though I was playing the 18th hole on the golf course, it was the first hole of sudden death against Fuzzy Zoeller. On the 72nd hole of the tournament I had played what I thought was a good, safe shot to the middle of the elevated green. As I walked up the hill to view my shot I realized the ball had come to rest in the back fringe, leaving me an impossible putt. The resulting three shots I took to finish my final round put me in a playoff with Fuzzy. We were to play the 18th once again.

Of all the courses and golf holes I've played through the years there may not be another hole with as much atmosphere. The 18th green is nestled at the bottom of a natural amphitheatre and sitting right on top of you are 20,000 plus golf fans. And when it's sudden death all eyes are on just that hole and the competitors. Determined not to make the same mistake again, I played to the front part of the green making sure to leave myself an uphill putt. But I over compensated and left myself 50 plus feet up a severe slope. Fortunately for me Fuzzy's ball came to rest just outside of mine and on the same line. It was such a difficult putt I actually thought two putts might be good enough for a win because of the severity of the green. Anyone who made the mistake of leaving their first putt above the hole was going to be in real trouble. Playing first, Fuzzy hit a really good putt just below and slightly left of the hole. It was close enough for him to finish. He was in with four. That really helped me focus, because I knew it would take a par four to continue and a birdie three to win. Best of all I had the perfect read, speed and line. I knew the putt would break slightly from right to left. With puts of this magnitude, the real challenge is to hit the putt dead solid, if you don't you could be in for real problems. As soon as I hit the putt, my first goal was accomplished….Dead Solid. As I looked up, I remember the ball rolling on the exact line I had pictured. It seemed like in slow motion. The ball took the slight break from right to left and with 10 feet to go, it was headed for the center of the hole. My caddie and good friend, Bob Arft, removed the flag. I could tell by his reaction that he thought the ball was going in. The last five feet seemed to last forever…what a thrill as that putt found the center of the hole. After I landed back to earth from my gigantic vertical leap of about 24 inches, the roar of the gallery and the smiling face of my wife Paddy were there to greet me. Along with Fuzzy who warmly congratulated me and whispered something in my ear that makes me smile every time I recall the moment.

Mark McCumber & Associates
McCumber Golf Facility Management

Mark McCumber

Mark McCumber posted 10 victories on the PGA Tour, including some big ones—Doral, the Players Championship, the Tour Championship—and pocketed more than $5 million. McCumber, 52, who took up golf course design and broadcasting later in his career, overcame a spinal cord injury caused by a viral infection to join the Champions Tour in 2001.

NO MAJOR, NO PROBLEM: "I don't feel empty about it at all. My life wouldn't be any different if I had one of them, and I would not take a major or two over the five to seven quality wins that I have. Fifty years ago, for instance, you couldn't physically play in all four. So tell me how important the majors were back then? Jack Nicklaus, in my opinion, made them important. If I pulled off the shot where I hit a driver off the fairway at the 1987 PGA, I might have a Wanamaker Trophy. But I played in the Ryder Cup, the World Cup. I'm more than satisfied."

THE RIGHT PRIORITIES: "My schedule was centered around school plays, graduation, anniversaries. When I kept that balance is when I played better. I'd fly home Sunday night and go back Tuesday night. Except for the tournament in Phoenix, I even stopped playing the West coast when my kids got old enough to go to school. I felt real good when my kids told me that I never made them feel secondary, that they've loved the way they've grown up and the opportunities they've been provided. I don't think five more trophies would have added anything to my sense of happiness. I feel very blessed."

BONUS TIME: "I couldn't feel below my waist. At first, they thought I might have MS. I thought I might never play golf again, but that wasn't what concerned me the most. My big goal was to be healthy enough to play catch with my kid. One doctor wanted to do surgery, telling me there was a good chance of permanent paralysis. I'm so grateful that didn't happen, and that I can play golf. The way I see it, I'm on bonus time. I get paid to play golf and to show my son this wonderful life."

Steve Melnyk

Steve Melnyk, the 1969 U.S. Amateur champion and 1971 British Amateur winner, finished second five times on the PGA Tour. During his most effective year, 1982, he placed 47th on the money list. Melnyk, 57, an ABC golf commentator, has achieved great success in other pursuits.

DIFFERENT DEATH: "Would I have liked to have played better? Sure. But I was dealt a strange hand. I had an elbow injury, and 23 years later, I'm still in the broadcast business. I can't straighten it out today. I slipped on a cart path at the Phoenix Country Club right before the first round of the Phoenix Open. I was walking with Fuzzy Zoeller to the range. But I went into business and know that I accomplished more in business than perhaps I could have as a professional. I started a bank, built it up, and sold it. I built a golf development company and sold that. I've been very lucky. I don't live in the past."

GO GATORS!: "I was all set to go to Georgia Tech, and then, late in my senior year of high school, the Florida coach visited me, invited me down, and offered me a scholarship on the spot. It was a very good break. I bleed orange and blue. Steve Spurrier and I were in the same fraternity pledge class. I went to the Fiesta Bowl where Nebraska kicked our butt, and I was in New Orleans when we won the national championship."

WHAT'S THE HURRY?: "It frustrates me when I see these young men who say they're playing the U.S. Amateur, turning pro the next week, almost like it's an afterthought. I've had conversations with the USGA [the United States Golf Association] about what we can do to get these kids to remain an amateur and play the Walker Cup. I'm a big proponent of amateur golf. My drum may get smaller with each year, but I'm going to keep banging it if I can."

RIVERSIDE
GOLF
GROUP

September 4, 2002

Dear Ron:

I'm flattered to have been asked to offer my thoughts on this most interesting subject. When first asked to participate, I thought this would be an easy exercise. Surely, I could not only remember the best shot that I had played, but could easily do the same for one that I had seen. Wrong on both counts!

Perhaps I should qualify myself on the second matter... the best shot that I have seen struck. Ten years on the PGA Tour combined with 21 years as a golf announcer has provided me a rich landscape from which to draw. I believe I'm the only golfer in the history of the game to have played in both amateur majors, all four professional majors, and now broadcast all four majors. It's given me an interesting perspective.

My runners-up to the best shot witnessed would be the chip-in by Larry Mize on the 11th hole at the 1987 Masters to best Greg Norman in a sudden-death playoff. I was the announcer on the hole, and after having set up the shot and the risks involved, truly didn't believe that he could get his ball near the hole. The result was unlikely, improbable, and great theater. In Norman, you had the tragic hero once again the unwitting victim, and Mize, the hometown hero, forever etching his name in the game's history.

My second runner-up would be Roberto de Vicenzo. The shot occurred in the Brazil Open at the Gavea Club in Rio de Janeiro. The hole and the circumstances are unimportant, but I watched Roberto, at age 52, play a shot off the ground with a driver on a par five that was timeless in its execution. Here was a player who was one of the game's best ball strikers... who never got his due... effortlessly playing an incredibly shot as though it was nothing at all. For those who were not fortunate to have seen him play, missed one of the game's greats.

The best shot witnessed was that of Jack Nicklaus. I'm sure there are many who would include him in their list, but for me it was special. We were paired in the first round of the 1970 Masters, and after three holes I was two under, and Jack one over. The fourth hole at Augusta National is a 220-yard par three, with the flagstick far right... and on that particular day, the wind was left to right in our face. Having the honor, I hit a two iron, knowing full well that it was not enough to reach the green, but there was no way I was going to hit a fairway wood. My shot came up short.

Jack turned to his caddie, Willie Peterson, and said, "We've got to start making some birdies". I thought he was crazy... given the shot he was about to play. He chose a one iron, and the shot he hit, I can still see today. It was majestic...he struck it so well, the wind never touched it, it never left the flag, and came to rest barely a foot from the hole. He never said a word, never look surprised... just handed Willie the one iron and walked off the tee as though what he just did was no big deal. I was in awe... and knew then that not only was he in a class by himself, but that the gap between him and "us" was pretty large.

As for my best shot, it pales by comparison, but the circumstances make it interesting. I'll try to set the scene:

It was the final round of the 1969 US Amateur at Oakmont... fourth hole, par five, and I'm in the right greenside bunker in two shots. I'm paired with Vinny Giles and hold a three shot lead. I walk into the bunker to look at the shot and look up to see Arnold Palmer in the gallery watching me! (I later found out he drove over from nearby Latrobe just to support the event). I was stunned and somewhat intimidated by his presence...not to mention very nervous. The flag was on the far left side of the green... I was about 100 feet away. Well, I holed the shot....made eagle 3, and coasted from there to win the Championship. The shot was good, the circumstances were unique, and the outcome was pretty special.

If you ask me in five years to take part in a similar exercise, in all likelihood, the best shots witnessed will probably change. I never cease to be amazed at the skill level across the board... from juniors to college to the Tour... the athleticism that is part of the game, combined with the fearlessness with which they seem to play, only promises to raise the bar. I hope I'm there to witness it!

Best regards,

Steven N. Melnyk

GAYLORD SPORTS
MANAGEMENT

Dear Michael,

The best shot I've ever hit came on the 17th at Valderrama in the 1997 Ryder Cup. Tom Lehman and I were even in a best-ball match against Ignacio Garrido and Jose Maria Olazabal. We were the last match of the day left on the course and at that point the Europeans were leading 4 & 3 because Nick Faldo and Lee Westwood had just won their match on 16 in front of us.

On the par-5, I drove it in the right rough and with the pin tucked two yards over the water I had 247 to the front of the green, 249 to the hole. That's a green that slopes severely from back to front. Hit the approach long and you're in a back bunker with almost no way to stop a shot in front of the green. Short, and you're down the bank and into the water. Even if you lay up, it can be hard to hold that green with a sand wedge and it was getting late in this key match.

I had an uphill lie in the first cut of rough and hit a 2-iron straight up in the air. As luck would have it, it was right at the hole, carried 248 and ended up 7 feet above the hole for eagle.

Also, as luck would have it, Garrido made a marvelous up-and-down with an 18-foot birdie putt to halve the hole. I didn't make my eagle putt, it horseshoed and came right back at me. But that 2-iron second shot was the greatest shot I ever hit.

Sincerely,

Phil Mickelson

Phil Mickelson

With his superb shot-making ability and go-for-broke mentality, Phil Mickelson has been one of the game's most charismatic players since he turned professional in the early 1990s. Mickelson, 33, the 1990 U.S. Amateur champion, has won 21 times, with four Ryder Cup appearances, and has earned more than $23 million. Mickelson is the most recent amateur to win a PGA Tour event, the 1991 Northern Telecom Open.

A LEFT TURN: "As a toddler, I mirrored what my right-handed father was doing as he hit balls at the family home, and learned to play that way. My father was my instructor. I bat left-handed and do virtually everything else right-handed. I used cut-down clubs when I was a kid and never had any problem getting the kind of equipment that I needed. People often ask me if a certain golf course might favor a left-handed or a right-handed player. But all it really means is that I might have to hit a fade on a certain shot when somebody else needs to hit a draw."

FAVORITE ATHLETES: "Muhammad Ali. I was too young to remember his boxing live, but I watch all the old tapes and highlights of his bouts. The real reason he's my favorite athlete is the way he was able to transcend the sport of boxing and appeal to everyone in the entire world. He took that opportunity and made the most of it in the way he's helped millions of people in the course of his life."

HOLY TOLEDO: "It's always been a dream of mine to pitch in a pro baseball game. Many guys on tour enjoy hunting or fishing in their off time, but I've always enjoyed more active pursuits. I believe baseball helps strengthen the proper golf muscles. A rotator cuff injury would be disastrous for a golfer, and this is helpful in preventing that as well as creating strength in my right side to help pull the golf club through faster. I incorporate baseball into my daily routine and I thought in my off time I'd take advantage of the opportunity to pursue a dream."

LARRY MIZE

August 18, 2003

Dear Mr. Arkush,

The greatest shot I ever hit was my chip shot to win the Masters on the 11th hole at Augusta National. I was born and raised in Augusta and had worked at the Masters' third hole scoreboard when I was a teenager. This made the tournament extra special for me. The 1987 tournament was my fourth Masters, and I had birdied the 72nd hole to gain a spot in the playoff with Seve Ballesteros and Greg Norman.

The sudden death playoff began on the 10th hole where Seve made bogey and was eliminated. Greg and I went to the 11th tee, and both of our tee shots found the fairway. My second shot sailed well right of the green leaving me with a 140-foot chip shot. Norman, on the other hand, was on the right fringe about 60 feet away. The green sloped sharply away from me toward a pond on the far side. The greens were so firm that year that the only shot I had was to play a bump and run with my sand wedge. My plan was to land the ball short of the fringe and let it run down to the hole. The rye grass around the green was pretty sticky so I knew I had to hit an aggressive shot. I executed the shot perfectly, and the ball went in the hole.

Being in a playoff with Norman and Ballesteros, two of the best players in the world at the time, and to win a major tournament in my hometown, made the circumstances surrounding the shot all that more exciting and special to me.

Sincerely,

Larry Mize

Larry Mize

Larry Mize

In the spring of 1987, Larry Mize upset superstars Greg Norman and Seve Ballesteros in a sudden-death playoff to win the Masters. The local boy was a national hero. As a teenager, Mize manned the scoreboard at Augusta National's third hole. He went on to attain two more victories, both in 1993. Mize, 45, has played regularly on the PGA Tour since 1982.

GEORGIA ON MY MIND: "The 1972 Masters was special, with Jack Nicklaus, my hero, winning, as was 1973, when Tommy Aaron won on Monday. I was working the scoreboard that year, and on Sunday, for some reason, I was the only one on the third hole. I had the headphones on and was sitting in the rain. It was kind of neat. It was a big deal to work there."

NEW EXPECTATIONS, NEW DOORS: "For the next few years after I won, I did not play as well. I put a little too much pressure on myself, had too many expectations, and that was a lesson I had to learn. You do not change things. You have to continue to do what you have done. As for the financial effect, winning has been very rewarding for me. All kinds of doors opened. Even today, I continue to reap the benefits of being a Masters champion, from opportunities to play in tournaments to participating in outings."

FAMILY FIRST: "My family comes before my career, and that is the way it has always been. People are going to think of me as a Masters champion. That is fine, but what I think is much more important is: Was I a Christian man? Was I a good father? Was I a good husband? I would like to think the answer is yes in all three cases."

BOB MURPHY, Inc.

A MOST MEMORABLE SHOT — PERHAPS LACKING THE CONNOTATION OF "GREAT" BECAUSE IT WAS NOT PLAYED UNDER TERRIFIC PRESSURE — WAS A DOUBLE EAGLE ON #2 AT PEBBLE BEACH IN 1972.

I AM FIRST OFF THE TEE IN SUNDAY'S LAST ROUND OF THE CROSBY. SEVEN THIRTY A.M. AND FOGGY, WET AND COLD, I BOGEYED #1, AS I HAD DONE ALL WEEK. THEN, ON THE PAR 5 SECOND HOLE I HIT A GOOD DRIVE. 239 YARDS REMAINING TO THE HOLE, I HIT A 3 WOOD (YES, WOOD) STRAIGHT AT THE HOLE AND WATCHED IT BOUNCE DEAD TO THE PIN. IT ROLLED UP THE GREEN AND DISAPPEARED! DOUBLE EAGLE!

BOTH PEOPLE IN MY GALLERY WERE CHEERING. ONE — GAIL WHO WAS VERY PLEASED WITH HER HUSBAND, THE OTHER — JOHN BRODIE WHO MUTTERED SOMETHING ABOUT 'LUCK OF THE IRISH'. IT SURE WAS —

Bob Murphy

Bob Murphy, the 1965 U.S. Amateur champion, was a steady performer on the PGA Tour throughout the late 1960s and early 1970s, winning five events. The best was yet to come. As a senior, he has captured 11 titles, finishing in the Top 30 on the money list every season from 1993 through 1998. Murphy, 61, shuttles between the Champions Tour and working as a golf commentator for NBC.

ON SECOND THOUGHT: "The Amateur was the turning point in whether I would be playing golf in the future, a statement to me that I could play with the best amateurs in the country and that I should think of the possibility of a career. Before that, I was just working on getting out of college and thinking about a job. I was going to be a high school coach. It was sort of a tainted victory in some ways because Bob Dickson had an extra club in his bag on Saturday and was assessed a two-shot penalty. However, he had the lead two or three times after that. He had his chance to win."

MAJOR MISTAKES: "I three-putted three times on the back nine, and I can go a year without three-putting three times. That cost me the 1969 Open at Champions. The 1975 Open at Medinah was another hard loss. Playing the last hole, I hit a four-wood off the tee because it was a sharp, dogleg right with a big mound that ran across the fairway. The ball hit the mound and bounced way left into the rough, my first unplayable lie since 1968. I finished one shot out of the playoff. That was a heart-breaker."

LESSONS FROM THE TOWER: "I learned that guys who win tournaments miss a lot of shots during the course of the week, and I learned that my patience was not good. I would think, how could a guy hit a shot like that and not get upset? Which, of course, I would do. If you look up the word *patience* in an Irish dictionary, it's not in there."

Terry-Jo Myers

LPGA veteran Terry-Jo Myers is a champion in more ways than one. Myers has battled back from interstitial cystitis, a bladder disease that almost ended her career. Finally, in the late 1990s, a new drug changed everything. Myers, 41, has posted three victories since joining the LPGA Tour in 1986. Her best season came in 1997, when she won two tournaments and finished 22nd on the money list.

KEEPING THE FAITH: "I went to the bathroom 50, 60 times a day, 70, 80 times a night, for almost 12 years. I overcame everything because of my faith—the same faith that I didn't always trust throughout those 12 years. I never asked why. I was always raised that you don't ask why. Bad things happen to people. But, at the same time, I would be so angry and bitter through periods of those years. Why did I have to suffer? I would let my anger come between my faith and myself."

A MOTHER'S LOVE: "After 10 years, I didn't know if I could do it any longer. It was not only the chronic pain that I was in; I was losing my career and everything else. Suicide seemed like an option versus living another 50 years in that kind of pain. For about a two-year period, I would get my car up to well over 100 miles per hour, praying I had enough strength to run it into a tree. But I never did. I pulled a knife out of my kitchen one morning, and the only thing that stopped me was going down the hall to say goodbye to my three-year-old daughter. She was sleeping. I looked at her and realized I could not leave her without a mother."

GIVING BACK: "I will continue to speak passionately about [interstitial cystitis]. Yesterday, I had four talks to give from 6 a.m. to 10:30 at night. I give 30 or 40 speeches a year, and I've spent five years lobbying Congress. Without question, I feel I am one of the most blessed people on this planet. I have become such a strong person."

Terry-Jo Myers
LPGA Member

Dear Michael,   9/10/03

        The shot I will always remember came on the final day of the 1997 Los Angeles Women's Championship at Oakmont Country Club in Glendale Ca. On the 16th hole after my drive went too far through the fairway, I ended up behind a tree, about 132 yards to the pin. If I chose to go under the tree, I could maybe chip it out and get it to the front part of the green where I could then chip onto the green. Another option was to try to hit it over the tree with a 9 iron by opening the blade, and hitting it as hard and as high as I possibly could. A perfect shot would get on the green. What was I to do.

        The television commentator was sure, even if I wasn't. "She's got to go under, she has no choice" she said.

        Yes, I did. I had to go for it, especially with Annika Sorenstam chasing me. Especially with what I had been through in recent years. Especially when I was allowed only one outcome. Victory. I hadn't been in contention in years, and I wasn't sure how many more opportunities I would get. I couldn't waste it. In any case,

Terry-Jo Myers
LPGA Member

I never believed in taking the easy way out.
A perfect shot it was. I stayed close
and chose it an hard as I could. The ball
cleared the tree, and finished twenty-four feet from
the hole. I knew it was pure from the
minute I hit it. As I walked up 18
a while later, I could it hold back the tears.
I knew I was going to win, and I knew
how much it meant to me. If I hadn't pulled
off the shot at 16, that triumph would may
never have happened.

Sincerely,

Terry-Jo Myers

Byron Nelson

August 30, 2001

Dear Dr. Cherney:

Thank you for your kind letter and please excuse my delay in answering. It's so embarrassing to find wonderful letters such as yours left on my usually cluttered desk for so long.

The greatest shot I ever saw was Gene Sarazen's double eagle at the fifteenth hole at Augusta National in the 1935 Masters. I was playing the seventeenth and had pushed my drive to the right, so I had to wait for Sarazen and his gallery to go past before I could proceed. So I had a perfect view of his shot and actually saw his ball go in the hole, and it was pretty exciting.

As for my own game, probably the best or at least most impressive shot was holing a 220-yard one-iron for an eagle two at the fourth hole in the second 18-hole playoff for the U.S. Open at the Spring Mill course at Philadelphia Country Club in 1939. It didn't make my opponent, Craig Wood, fold up on the spot, but I had the impression that it definitely did get his attention.

Best wishes with your project.

Sincerely,

Byron

Byron Nelson

Byron Nelson

Along with Ben Hogan and Sam Snead, Byron Nelson belonged to the game's magical triumvirate in the 1930s, '40s, and '50s, setting records and standards for future generations. In 1945, Nelson set one record that will always be out of reach—18 victories, including an incredible 11 in a row. A year later, Nelson retired to his ranch in Roanoke, Texas. At 92, he remains the game's most respected ambassador.

THE STREAK: "After a fine year in 1944, I made a little change. Not in my swing. I had kept a detailed account of my tournaments, and when I checked it before 1945, I found two things were in there frequently. One was 'careless shot,' the other, 'poor chipping.' Those two were in there much more than anything else. So I made up my mind that, in 1945, I would not play a careless shot. I know that sounds silly, but sometimes you can hit it without thinking. You have to think about every single shot, every single putt. The first time that I had interviews about [the streak] was when I won the PGA, which was the ninth one."

HOGAN: "The relationship has been exaggerated. They've talked about us caddying together. I caddied at the same course, but I never caddied in a group with Ben and I didn't caddie long. I was soon working in the golf shop, and then I mowed the greens. I saw him on the rare occasion, but I didn't get acquainted with him until the late 1930s. I was outgoing, talking to people all the time, and he wasn't doing any of that. Strangers made him nervous. I was never in Hogan's home, and I don't think he was ever in mine."

THEY EARNED IT: "People say the players are making too much money, and I say that's not true. If they are, then all of the other top athletes are making too much. Nobody gives them a putt. Nobody gives them anything. You're not on a team. If you have a bad day, well, you have a bad day. If you are on a team, the team might still win."

Bobby Nichols

Bobby Nichols has his share of triumphs, highlighted by the 1964 PGA Championship when he outdueled Arnold Palmer and Jack Nicklaus. Nichols, an 11-time winner on the PGA Tour, has also gone through his share of trials. In high school, a car accident put him in the hospital for three months. In 1975, he was struck by lightning during the Western Open. Nichols, 68, plays occasionally on the Champions Tour.

A BOLT, NOT TOMMY: "It was a typical overcast day in Chicago. All of a sudden, the lightning came. Back in those primitive days, we didn't have warnings that lightning was in the area. The bolt knocked me and the standard bearer to the ground while we were walking up the fourth fairway. Startled more than anything else, we looked at each other and took off running as fast as we could toward the tent, which was probably 150 yards away. We were taken to the hospital. I had to withdraw from the tournament. Someone asked me what my wife thought, and I said, 'She thinks I'm more electrifying.' Whenever I play now, I'm very aware of inclement weather. Florida is the lightning capital of the world. When the lightning gets around me, I'm one of the first to head for shelter."

DOWN AND UP: "I was unconscious after the car accident for 13 days, and during that period of time, they told my mom that there was a possibility I would never walk again. I had a broken pelvis, internal injuries, a brain concussion, and a broken wrist. I was paralyzed from the waist down. But, luckily, things worked out. Someone must have been watching over me, I figure."

THE OTHER BEAR: "I went to Texas A&M on a football scholarship, but all I did was play golf. My coach was a good friend of Coach Bryant, who was also the athletic director. Coach Bryant could do anything he wanted. He was tough, but very fair. I played in celebrity pro-ams with him. His golf game was nothing like his coaching. I'd say he was an A+ in coaching and probably an 18-plus handicapper on the golf course."

VIP
SPORTS MANAGEMENT, INC.

November 6th, 2000

Dear Ron:

Thanks for your interest in some of golf's most memorable shots, as witnessed by the tour players themselves. I'm sure it will make for an interesting read!

As you know, I've been a touring professional for over 40 years, and have seen my share of miraculous and not so miraculous shots. However, after some thought, these three come to mind.

My most memorable shot:

In 1964 I was fortunate enough to win the PGA Championship, and as most players that have won will tell you, there is usually one shot that was a turning point in the tournament for them. Mine was during the final round at the par 5 tenth hole. I was paired with Tom Neiporte and the legendary Ben Hogan, and was leading the event by one shot at the time. Nicklaus and Palmer were in the group in front of me, and they were both making a charge. Tom and Mr. Hogan had both laid up their second shots, and I was debating on what to do. This particular hole was the type that if I hit the green it would be an easy four, yet if I missed the green, it could be a hard six! Being young and nieve, I went for the green and it paid off. I hit it approximately 30 feet left of the hole and made the putt for eagle. This put me ahead by three, which was my eventual winning margin over Jack and Arnold. What made this shot even more memorable was the comment Mr. Hogan made as he was congratulating me on 18. He said, "Bobby, I'm surprised you went for the green at ten. It was a risky shot, but it paid off for you." My reply was "thank you Mr. Hogan, I probably didn't know any better!" I played a number of rounds with Mr. Hogan during my career, and he was always gracious and helpful to me. Playing with him that final round helped keep my emotions under control.

Most memorable shot hit by a fellow competitor:

During one round of the Phoenix Open in the early '60's, Jack Nickluas hit a shot I will never forget. Jack, Gary Player, and myself were paired together. We were teeing of at the par 4 fourth hole at Phoenix Country Club. It was a reachable par for the long hitters (312 yds.), yet it was guarded by a bunker about 20 yards in front of the green. This was definitely not the place to hit your ball; so most players laid up with a 2 or 3 iron to give themselves a full pitch shot to the green. On this particular day, it had rained that morning and the ground was soft. I was first to hit and laid up with a three iron. Gary was next and he also laid up with a 2 or 3 iron. As we waited, Gary noticed Jack had pulled out his driver. He looked at me and said, "we've got him now!" Jack proceeded to hit a huge drive right at the green. After, Gary and I hit our approach shots, we noticed a ball plugged in the green about three feet from the hole. Jack calmly marked his ball, cleaned it, and tapped it in for an eagle two! Gary and I looked at each other and laughed. I then said, "yeah, we've got him now alright!"

Funniest shot:

As you can imagine, I've seen some funny shots over my career, most of which were hit by me! However, one of the funniest scenarios I can remember took place at the Bob Hope Desert Classic and it involved my good friend Gay Brewer and the NBC golf announcer Charlie Jones. We were on the 18th hole at Indian Wells C.C. and NBC had their trailers and equipment parked down the left side, along with some portable restrooms. Charlie was fairly new with NBC at the time and he was standing on the tee doing the roving report duties. Gay proceeded to pull his ball left and hit one of the portable restrooms on the fly, making a loud bang! We couldn't see where the ball went, so Charlie asked what the ruling was. I then calmly answered, "Charlie, it's a free drop, due to casual shit!" We all busted up laughing, especially Charlie, who was on the air at the time. I wasn't fined, so I'm sure it was edited out. I'm certainly no comedian, but that one just came to me.

Ron, I hope you find some entertainment in these shots and I thank you again for your interest. Best of luck with your book and I'll be sure to purchase a copy when it gets published!

Sincerely,

Bobby Nichols

Jack Nicklaus

Jack Nicklaus, 64, was the greatest golfer of the 20th century. Nicklaus started his remarkable run at the 1962 U.S. Open, capping it with his one-for-the-ages performance at the 1986 Masters. In between, the Golden Bear won everything that mattered. In the 1970s, he turned his attention to golf course design, another field he has mastered.

Three of his 18 professional major championships stand out from the pack. Following is a brief summary of each one:

1962 U.S. OPEN: Nicklaus, a rookie, was the enemy in those days. He possessed the audacity, after all, to challenge the beloved King, Arnold Palmer, on his territory, no less—Oakmont Country Club near Pittsburgh. Nicklaus, 22, absorbed all kinds of abuse that week, yet he held his emotions—and his game—together to defeat Palmer in the 18-hole playoff, 71 to 74.

1975 MASTERS: The moment everyone remembers is the 40-foot birdie putt on 16, and the exuberant reaction from both Nicklaus and his caddie, Willie Peterson. The birdie would be the difference, though Tom Weiskopf and Johnny Miller had chances to force a playoff. But both missed makeable birdie opportunites at 18—Miller from 20 feet, Weiskopf from 8 feet—allowing Nicklaus to claim his fifth green jacket and 13th major title.

1986 MASTERS: Jack wasn't supposed to be back, not at the age of 46, at Augusta National. In fact, a few days before the tournament, a writer for the *Atlanta Journal-Constitution* used phrases such as "washed up" and "done" to describe the Golden Bear. The article was put on the refrigerator at the house where Nicklaus was staying. On Sunday, after birdies at 10 and 11, Nicklaus bogeyed 12. He was running out of holes, but a birdie at 13, an eagle at 15, and birdies at 16 and 17 led to a back-nine 30. Tom Kite missed a 12-foot birdie attempt at 18 that would have forced a playoff.

Jack Nicklaus

October 3, 2003

Dear Ron:

Thank you for your recent note and your interest in my thoughts on which golf shot from my 50-plus years of playing this wonderful game I would call my greatest. That's a difficult question, for several reasons. I've hit a lot of shots that might be considered "great" but were ultimately unimportant to the outcome of a golf tournament. I may have a hit a great iron shot or made a long, breaking putt that was of no consequence in the end because the shot didn't enable me to win the tournament or put myself in position to win. To me, a great shot would be one that was significant to the outcome or netted the greatest result. For example, Tom Watson's chip-in for birdie on the 17th hole at Pebble Beach in the 1982 U.S. Open was one of the greatest shots I've seen because of what it meant to the final result. I wasn't playing with Tom at the time, so I didn't see it in person, but since it denied me a fifth U.S. Open, I saw so many replays of it that it seemed as though I saw it first-hand!

It is simply too tough for me to select _one_ shot in my career that proved to be the most critical to a victory or got the greatest result, but I can certainly think of a number of clutch shots that made me particularly proud or evoke a fond memory. I could go as far back as 1959, when I won my first national title in the U.S. Amateur at the Broadmoor Golf Club. On the 36th and final hole of my match with Charles Coe, with the match square, I hit a punch 9-iron that rolled back to the pin and to eight feet. I made the birdie putt to win my first of two U.S. Amateur titles. There was the 1967 U.S. Open at Baltusrol, when, playing with Arnold Palmer, I needed birdie on the 18th to break Ben Hogan's scoring record. I had a third shot to the par-5 finishing hole of 238 yards, but uphill, all carry, and against the wind, it played more like 260. I put all I had into a 1-iron, carried the ball over the corner of a greenside bunker, and put it to 22 feet for birdie and the record. There was the 1970 British Open at St. Andrews, when I drove the green at 18 (a 358-yard par 4) and actually hit it through. I had a tough pitch from the thick grass on the back bank but hit it to eight feet and made the putt to beat Doug Sanders. I remember erupting in celebration, tossing the putter in the air, and almost hitting poor Doug in the head.

As much as I love the U.S. Open and Pebble Beach, I'd have to include the 1-iron on the par-3 17th in 1972 that hit the flagstick and stopped just inches from the hole, virtually sealing my victory. In one of my favorite down-the-stretch duels, I was able to hold off Tom Weiskopf and Johnny Miller in the 1975 Masters, and perhaps the biggest shot in the final stretch was the 38-foot putt on the 16th hole. The image of me leaping into the air after the putt captured a moment that remains one of my most vivid memories, and when I opened my home club in Florida, The Bear's Club, we used that image in the logo. The same year, I had a 9-iron over the trees and pond on the 16th hole at Firestone that led to birdie and my PGA Championship win. There was 1980, at Baltusrol, when fans were chanting, "Jack's back! Jack's back!" My 22-foot birdie putt on the 17th hole was critical in holding off Isao Aoki and led to my fourth U.S. Open title. And, of course, in the final round of the 1986 Masters, at age 46 and with my son Jack on the bag, I had a 4-iron and eagle putt on 15 that were among several unforgettable moments in what I consider my most memorable tournament victory.

These are a few of the shots that I think produced some of the most important wins of my career. All of them were great to me, and to choose just one would diminish the others. Instead of *greatest shots* I would prefer to call them *snapshots* that make up my memories of a very rewarding career.

Good golfing,

GREAT WHITE SHARK ENTERPRISES, INC.

GREG NORMAN

May 12, 2003

Dear Michael:

In response to your question regarding which shot I believe was the greatest that I've hit in my career, I would have to say it came next to the 17th green, the "Road Hole" at St. Andrews.

I was playing in the Dunhill Cup and missed the green to the right over the road two feet from the wall, but on the grass. I was ahead in my match, and given the fact that I had no room for a back swing I felt the time was right for me to try and hit a bit of a risky shot. I calculated the launch angle to a fairly flat-faced rock in the wall that had what I thought was the proper angle to ricochet the ball onto the green.

I chose a 9-iron and hit the target on the wall and the ball rebound onto the green six feet from the hole. I went on to win the match.

Given the unusual type of shot this was, as well as the fact that it isn't a shot that you practice much, if ever, I feel that this was certainly one of the greatest shots I ever hit.

Best regards,

Greg Norman

/lma

Greg Norman

Australia's Greg Norman, the Shark, has been one of the game's most popular figures for more than 20 years. Norman has been a big winner on and off the course, with dozens of tournament titles and a wide assortment of successful business ventures. With two British Opens (1986, 1993) and three Vardon Trophy awards, Norman, 49, was inducted into the World Golf Hall of Fame in 2001.

"The greatest shot I ever saw him hit was during the Players Championship. At the par-5 16th, he hooked his drive into the woods. He then hooked a low two-iron out of the rough in the tree line, on to the green. It was one of those things that Arnold Palmer used to do. There was no great obstacle that he couldn't overcome. That was the nature of Greg Norman's game. He always wanted to take that extra chance and live on the razor's edge."—*Frank Chirkinian,* longtime producer of golf for CBS

"If there was a book about golf, encompassing everything, Greg Norman should probably be on the cover. So few people win, and even the greatest spend so little of their time winning. It's more about who you are and the kind of person you are when you lose. He lost with such grace and always showed up the next time with his chin up. He was still Greg Norman. It's rare to see someone endure what he endured in his career and still be great to the end. That would batter most people down." —*David Feherty*

"For over a decade, Greg Norman had a huge impact on the game of golf, even more so in Australia, where a whole generation of young men have grown up idolizing Greg, reading his books and watching him on TV, learning how to play his way. You look at all the great young Australian players, and you can owe all of that to Greg Norman's influence on them. He had more charisma than anyone else since Arnold Palmer."—*Ian Baker-Finch*

MS. SE RI PAK

July 23, 2003

I feel my greatest shot was at the 1998 Women's US Open on the 18th hole Monday
play-off against Jenny Chuasiriporn. My tee shot landed about one foot from the
water hazard, which ran along the entire left side of the 18th hole. When I got to my
ball, my first thought was I had no chance to hit it. I was thinking that's it, I have
lost the Championship. But when I realized it was the last hole on the last day, I
decided to try something. So I took off my shoes and socks and with the help of my
caddy, I climbed down into the water. Taking my stance, the water came halfway
up my calves. I had to focus hard on keeping a solid stance as well as concentrate
on putting the clubface on the ball, which was positioned well above my feet. I took
my A-wedge and chipped it out and across the fairway. From there, I was easily
able to get it on the green and two putt for a good bogey which ended up enabling
me to take the play-off into extra holes, whereby I eventually won on the 2nd extra
hole.

Se Ri Pak

Se Ri Pak made a tremendous impact from the start. As a rookie in 1998, she won four tournaments, including two majors, and finished second on the money list. Sophomore jinx? Not for Pak, who prevailed four more times in 1999. Rebounding from a substandard season in 2000, she captured 13 events over the next three years. Pak, 26, has spawned a wave of South Korean female golfers hoping to duplicate her success.

I HAVE A DREAM: "In 1997, when I played in the U.S. Open for the first time, I was saying to my mom how great it would be to win the Open someday. I started to dream of holding that trophy. When it did happen, I was surprised; I didn't expect it to come that fast. I was a baby, and it caused big changes in my life. I gained confidence and trust. On the other hand, I felt a lot of pressure on me, more than ever before. I had a really hard time with it for a while. The press in Korea thought I should win every week. I realized that I was pushing myself too hard. Once I stopped doing that, I played much better."

ON TRACK: "I started when I was about 9 or 10 years old, and did it for about seven years. I ran the 100 meters, the 100-meter hurdles. My best time was 13 seconds. When I was 12 years old, I dreamed about being an Olympic athlete. But, over time, I took it less seriously. I stopped when I was 15 so I could devote my time to golf. I still run a little, maybe 20 to 30 minutes, but only for exercise."

CAPTAIN VIDEO: "I used to play video games on the road a lot. When I go home, I play Nintendo golf or one of the Playstations. I have all the Game Boys. Playing video games relaxes me a little. You don't have to think about anything. You just have to play the game. It's good to have something like that away from the tour."

arn●ld palmer

August 29, 2003

Dear Ron:

The question you have posed is a very good one, but one
that is extremely difficult to answer. There have been
many memorable shots throughout my career that proved
pivotal to the outcome of a tournament. However, if I
were forced to choose only one, I would say it was the
three-wood shot that I hit to the green at the 13th hole in
the final round of the 1958 Masters.

I had just had a ruling dispute at the 12th hole, played
two balls and was awaiting word from the full Rules
Committee which one would count – a three, which I felt I
was entitled to, or a five, which would have dropped me
out of the tournament lead. I put my tee shot at 13 in the
middle of the fairway. With Bob Jones looking on, I was
determined to take the risk and go for the water-guarded
green on the par-five hole. I caught the ball perfectly. It
carried 20 feet past the hole and I sank the eagle putt.

I needed that eagle because, after the Rules Committee
advised me two holes later that I had made three at the
12th, I wound up winning my first Masters by a single
stroke over Doug Ford, the defending champion, and Fred
Hawkins.

Sincerely,

Arnold Palmer

Arnold Palmer

Forget the seven professional major championships and the 62 tournament victories. The real numbers that matter in the rise of Arnold Palmer, the son of a western Pennsylvania pro/greenskeeper, can't be added up—the army of millions he attracted in the early 1960s that helped golf become a major sport in America. He was, and remains, simply, the King. Palmer, 74, will play in his 50th straight Masters this spring.

FIFTY YEARS AGO: "Winning the 1954 National Amateur came at a point in my life when I was working as a manufacturer's rep and had just gotten out of the service. I had been playing pretty good golf, winning some local events. When I won the Amateur, it gave me the perspective I was looking for. I was confident that if I decided to turn pro, I could do it without any problem, and I did shortly after that."

THE DRIVE IN DENVER: "I hit a couple of balls on the practice tee [in the 1960 U.S. Open at Cherry Hills] to get loosened up to start the afternoon round. My whole thought was getting off to a quick start. The potential was there for making some birdies. The one thing that came right to my mind [on the par-4 opening hole in the final round] was the fact that, on the first day, I drove it in the ditch to the right. This time I made a pretty good swing and knocked the ball on the green. I got so excited, I almost three-putted."

ME AND THE BEAR: "I value Jack's friendship very much. He came along at a time when things were going very well for me. I tried to help him get started as a pro, and I'm very pleased with that, and the fact that Barb and Jack were very close friends of mine and Winnie's. We played a lot of championships as a team and played against each other as competitively as you could ever do anything. When my wife died, Barb was one of the people that gave me the help that I needed to get on with my life."

JERRY PATE COMPANY

July 3, 2002

Dear Ron:

Without a doubt, the most memorable shot I have struck was the 5 iron to win the 1976 U. S. Open at the Atlanta Athletic Club. My fellow competitor, John Mahaffey had just three putted the 17th to give me a one shot lead. His tee shot found the rough on 18. He attempted an heroic 4 wood shot to reach the green, which sadly found the water. I also drove my ball into the right hand rough, coming to rest on top of the thick Bermuda grass.

My second shot to the 18th, approximately 190 yards to the flagstick, seemed certain to be a 4 iron. But my caddy, John Considine convinced me I was pumped up and the ball would carry longer with a flyer lie. Without hesitation, I trusted his judgment and with the confidence of any cocky 22 year old rookie, hit the shot perfectly to the flagstick. It came to rest only two feet away, which assured a birdie 3 and a 2 shot victory.

Not only was this the greatest shot of my career, but it was the start of my many wonderful memories in professional golf.

Sincerely,

JERRY PATE

JP:pm

Jerry Pate

In 1976, Jerry Pate was no ordinary tour rookie, winning both the U.S. Open and the Canadian Open. Pate won eight times in all, including the 1982 Tournament Players Championship, which he celebrated by shoving Commissioner Deane Beman and architect Pete Dye into the lake by the 18th green. Pate, 50, plagued by shoulder injuries throughout his career, is a rookie again—on the Champions Tour.

A SWIM, ANYBODY?: "Deane was spontaneous, Pete Dye was not. To bring a little levity to the game, I thought it would be a light touch to not only throw Pete in, but to throw the commissioner in. I said to Deane, 'Come over here a minute. I want to show you something by this lake that you need to fix.' He walked over there, and all of a sudden, I grabbed him and threw him in. He thought it was great."

ORANGE BALL: "I was working for Wilson Sporting Goods back in the early 1980s, and they thought it was a great marketing idea to have someone play the colored ball. I thought it would be a great conversation piece, plus I got paid a lot of money to use it. They paid me bonuses for wins with it. I stopped using it in the mid-1980s."

ALWAYS MARK WITH TAILS: "One day Tom Weiskopf asked me if I was superstitious, and I said, 'No,' and he said, 'You got to either mark your ball on heads or tails. You need to mark it the same way every time.' I kind of blew it off and then started thinking about it. When I was playing football in elementary school, I was one of the captains. We would flip to see who had field position. Our coach always told us to call tails. His motto was: 'Tails never fails.' That's where it started."

Calvin Peete

The greatest shot I ever hit was the shot on no.17 at the
Tournament Players Club at Sawgrass the final round in
1985 the year I won The Players Championship. When I
walk on the tee my knees where shaking. I barely had
control of my emotions. I selected my club. An eight iron, I
had to tell myself, "Calvin this is what you have been
hitting all those balls for, this Shot!" And I hit the shot
about 3 1/2 feet of the pin. After I hit the shot all I could
do is take a sip of water and proudly take the walk up to
17th green and make the putt!

The greatest shot I ever saw was at the Tradition in
Scottsdale AZ. at Desert Mountain. I was new to the Sr. Tour
known as the Champions Tour to date I was playing with
Tom Shaw a past champion of the Tradition no. 11 a par 5.
Tom was all over the place on the hole when he go to the
green he chipped it by   on his 3rd shot, his 4th
shot was short, his 5th shot in the HOLE! for a great par.
Tom told the fans following, "Folks don't try this at home,
this is par the hard way". We all had a good laugh and
went to the next hole.

Calvin Peete

Calvin Peete didn't learn how to play golf until he was 23 years old, but made up for lost time in a hurry. Between 1979 and 1986, Peete, one of 19 children, won 12 tournaments, including four in 1982. He rarely missed a fairway, leading in driving accuracy an unprecedented 10 years in a row. Since 2001, Peete, 60, has worked on the teaching staff at the PGA Tour Golf Academy in Florida.

SAVED BY GOLF: "I sold wares to migrant workers—clothes, jewelry, pots, pans, whatever they wanted. The migrant camps were a long ways from town. I would go into the cities and buy things from the wholesale houses and take them back to the camps and sell them to the workers. Golf saved me. It kept me out of the streets for one thing. I was still in the streets, even though I was trying to be an entrepreneur. I was hanging around the pool room, the gambling houses, and so forth."

SMITTEN FROM THE START: "I had been hanging around with these guys, playing basketball and softball with them. They wanted me to go to the golf course, but golf, to me, seemed to be a very silly game. So I would always tell them some excuse. They came by the motel one day and said there was a clambake in the park, a bunch of people getting together, cooking clams, frying fish, drinking beer, playing loud music. I had gone to one or two of them before and had a great time. Instead, we ended up on the golf course. They said, 'You either play golf or sit here in the car, and wait until we finish.' I rented a set of clubs, and I've been hooked ever since."

NO ELBOW ROOM: "I fell out of a tree when I was 12 years old. I was picking cherries. I've had the elbow x-rayed by a couple of leading orthopedic surgeons and they say it's a good elbow, and if it doesn't bother me, don't bother with it. It didn't bother me, as far as my golf was concerned. I still had a good golf swing. I just didn't have the extension, where I could have hit the ball much longer."

Gary Player
GROUP

I was playing in The Tradition, a major tournament on the Champions Tour at Desert Mountain Golf Course in Arizona with Jack Nicklaus and Arnold Palmer (The Big Three). We came to the 7th hole - a par three. It was a double green, shared with the 15th hole, just like so many at St. Andrews... one big green. On the tee, which was highly elevated, with the wind behind us, I took a 6 iron and knocked the ball right into the cup! Then, we played around the rest of the way and came back to the same green, this time on the 15th hole – a par 5. I managed to hold a wedge shot for my 3rd. So, I had 2 eagles in the same round on the same green. Lyle Anderson, the owner and developer, kindly put a plaque on the back of the green saying "Gary Player is the only man to eagle the 7th and the 15th in the same round." I'd say that was probably my most interesting hole-in-one shot and I've had over 20 during competition in my career.

Of course with my wife, Vivienne, having had two holes-in-one in the same round (which she keeps reminding me about), I have had this on my mind and have always wanted to achieve this myself. After my two eagles on this day, we came to the 17th hole, which is a par 3. I hit my shot and the ball actually went right around the cup and stopped on the edge. I would have given anything to go to my wife and tell her than I also had two holes-in-one in the same round, but it just never worked out!

Remember, the harder you practice, the luckier you get!

GARY PLAYER

GP/gc

Gary Player

South Africa's Gary Player came to the United States in the late 1950s . . . and he conquered. One of only five golfers in the history of the game to capture all four major championships, Player has nine overall, including three Masters titles and three British Opens. Player, 68, has gone everywhere, logging more than 14 million miles. He served as captain of the International squad during last year's Presidents Cup matches.

FREQUENT FLYER: "I used to travel with my wife and six children, with 33 pieces of baggage, and have three bedrooms and three taxis. So when I travel on my own now, I just make a comparison, and it's so much easier. But it's not easy. I love to be on my ranch in South Africa with my thoroughbred racehorses. To be living in motels is quite an adjustment when you come from the ranch and Sunday afternoon lunches with your family. But that's the life I have chosen and I'm very grateful for it."

FITNESS FANATIC: "Being of small stature, golfwise, it helped me tremendously. In my 50 years, there's never been a human being who has had the schedule like I've had. The fitness has allowed me to do that, to compete against the bigger guys and beat them. I go to the gym five times a week and try to do 1,000 crunches with an 80-pound weight on my chest. I push a lot of heavy weights with my legs and arms, and do some running on the treadmill. But the big thing is how you eat. The United States is the most incredible country but has the worst eaters on the planet."

MAN IN BLACK: "My father said to me: 'If you're going to be a world champion, you've got to have a trademark. You're from black Africa. Why don't you wear black and have a Black Knight emblem?' It started in the late 1950s. On cool days, black is 11 degrees hotter than, say, white. So I wore black, and it made it a lot warmer, no question about it."

Judy Rankin

Longtime ABC on-course commentator Judy Rankin, a 26-time tour winner, was inducted into the World Golf Hall of Fame in 2000. Rankin put together her most productive years in 1976 and 1977, winning 11 tournaments and back-to-back money titles. In 1976, she became the first professional female golfer to earn more than $100,000 in a single season. Rankin, 59, was captain of the victorious 1996 and 1998 U.S. Solheim Cup teams.

OPEN FEARS: "I was always intimidated at the U.S. Open. When I played well, I had command of the situation, but I never had command at the Open. From the time I was 8, I considered the USGA events bigger than life, and that didn't change once I got older. Adding to the whole situation was the fact that I came from ordinary circumstances, and the Open is almost always played at a very elite country club with an elite crowd. I'd work so hard that by the time I teed off, I was so exhausted. Everyone in my family was in a complete knot. I played well in three or four of them, but I played poorly in a lot more."

SOLHEIM SATISFACTION: "I loved it. It was almost like being in college, an experience I never had. I learned that I had the ability to motivate people, to make sense out of the chaos in their lives once in a while. I got more wrapped up in the event than in any individual tournament I ever played. Maybe it's better to be wrapped up in other people instead of yourself. If there were a full-time job like that, I'd love to have it."

CHANGING TIMES: "When I was a child, there were either rules against young children playing or, as young people came along, they made rules to make it an adult event. When there were one or two kids, it was an oddity. Now, it's accepted, and most women are very supportive. There were two women who were very special, who befriended me. I haven't seen either one since I was 25 years old, though. I remember their names and what they did."

July 12, 2003

I'm not sure I can actually remember my best shot any longer! It was 1952, I was 7 years old. The St. Louis Post-Dispatch newspaper sponsored an annual hole-in-one contest at the third hole of a little nine hole club in Forest Park, Triple A. The course became the place I would learn to play with the help of my father and professional Bob Green. At this point I had hit a lot of balls for nearly a year, but had barely been on a course.

Late in the afternoon, as people went home from work, quite a crowd would gather. Both to hit balls and to watch. The par 3 was about 110 yards.

JUDY RANKIN

You got to hit three balls. I teed up my driver, calmly put three in a row on the green (I think), and won the women's division for closest to the hole! It was my first experience with the press. I wasn't very savvy. In a radio interview I continually shook my head yes and no to questions. I've probably talked enough over the years to make up for that ten-fold.

There have been others that were harder, more dramatic, and memorable. This first one, though, may have had a great bearing on the rest.

Judy Rankin

Chi Chi Rodriguez
Management Group, Inc.

Dear Michael:

My greatest shot is an easy one to remember. It occurred in the 1991 U.S. Senior Open at Oakland Hills Country Club just outside Detroit. I was chasing Jack Nicklaus. Who wasn't? On the final hole, I needed a birdie to get into an 18-hole playoff the next day. I thought I had a birdie the hole before but somehow my 10-footer didn't drop. In the fairway at 18, I was now about 175 yards from the green.

My caddie wanted me to hit a five iron, but, being a low ball hitter, I knew that if I hit a 5 iron, I would not be able to stop the ball on the green. The green was simply too hard. But if I hit a 6 iron straight, the ball would probably plug in the trap, ruining any real chance I'd have for that birdie. There was only one option: Take a six iron and try to hook it. I played the shot in my brain before I hit it, and it worked out the exact same way that I had pictured it. I aimed at the right trap, hooked it 50 yards, and the ball headed toward the green. From the moment I hit it, I knew it would be stiff. It stopped about a foot and a half from the cup. My caddie came over to help me read it. "You just want to get on TV," I told him. "Get out of here."

I only wish I could have played someone else in the playoff, anybody besides Jack Nicklaus. I played good; he played great. He played like Jack Nicklaus, shooting 65 to beat me by four strokes. Truth is, though, that I didn't really care if I won or I lost. I was just happy to be in the playoff, to be in the company of the greatest player in the world, to have pulled off the shot I needed at the time I needed it most.

Sincerely,

Chi Chi Rodriguez

Chi Chi Rodriguez

Chi Chi Rodriguez

Juan "Chi Chi" Rodriguez will turn 70 in 2005, but his act will never grow old. For more than four decades, Chi Chi has cracked up galleries all over the world with his sword dance and one-liners. Chi Chi has also received good reviews for his performance between the ropes, with 30 victories, including 22 on the Champions Tour. Seven came in 1987, when he was the tour's leading money winner.

THE MOTHER: "About 20 years ago, President Marcos asked me who I wanted to meet, the Pope or Mother Teresa. I told him, 'We'll always have another Pope.' I prayed the night before, and I said, 'God, if she is an angel, show me.' When I shook her hand, every hair on my body stood up. It was the most electrifying time of my life. I felt the power of God in her. The first thing she told me was, 'You are rich. How come you don't share with the poor?' I had a check in my hand and gave it to her. I spent 45 minutes with her. When I saw her go away in the airplane, I started crying like a baby."

THE MATADOR: "When I was a kid, I was playing someone for five cents. I made a putt from about 15 feet, but there was a toad in the hole. The toad hopped out and there came my ball. The kid said the putt is no good until it hits the bottom of the hole. My ball never did hit the bottom. After that, I started putting my hat over the hole. Some of the pros complained that I was damaging the hole. That's when I thought of the matador routine."

BASEBALL WAS BERRY, BERRY GOOD: "I probably could throw it faster than Sandy Koufax. You can ask [former professional golfer] Ken Still about that. But one day, I saw future major leaguer Darryl Spencer hit home runs at Ft. Sill, Oklahoma. I started worrying. People couldn't hit me, but if a guy like that were to hit a line drive at me, he'd probably kill me. I never weighed over 117 pounds."

DOUG SANDERS

March 5, 2002

RE: Greatest golf shot story for Ron Cherney's book

The greatest golf shot that I have ever hit was without a doubt on the 17th hole at St. Andrews in the final round of the British Open in 1970.   The 17th hole is better known as the "road hole", with one of the most feared green side bunkers in all of golf. The general public may not remember my great shot, because unfortunately, most people only remember the 3-putt on the 18th hole, which cost me the title.

On the final day, I hit a good tee shot up the fairway leaving myself with a 4-iron onto the green. The wind was blowing from right to left, and my second shot ended up on the down slope, in the bunker on the left, short of the green. The odds were very heavily against me that I could get the ball within 12-15 feet of the hole. However, if I could manage to somehow make Par, the 18th hole was down wind and should have been an easy hole to Par to win my first Major Championship.

I had won 18 previous tournaments without one of them being a Major, and I cannot recall anyone else having won that many tournaments and still not win a Major.

Walking into the bunker, I knew that this was going to be one of the most difficult shots to execute. I came within 2 feet of the hole and I made it in for Par. It was one of those beautiful shots that you seem to hit once in a lifetime. It would have gone down in history as the shot that won Doug Sanders the British Open if I had not 3-putted the 18th hole.

Jack Nicklaus later said "it was the greatest bunker shot he had ever seen in a Major tournament".

But that is life, and one has to continue with the good and the bad....and the game of golf has certainly brought me a lot more good than bad.

Doug Sanders

Doug Sanders

Nobody in the game was more colorful than Doug Sanders. There wasn't an outfit he wouldn't wear. He could also be dazzling on the course, with 20 PGA Tour victories, including the 1956 Canadian Open, which he won as an amateur. In the 1970 British Open at St. Andrews, Sanders missed a short putt on the 72nd green that would have given him the Claret Jug. At 70, he remains as flashy as ever.

THE PUTT: "Somebody said, 'How often do you think about the putt?' I said, 'I don't think about it that much. Sometimes I go as long as five minutes without thinking about it.' I'm joking, of course, but it comes up a lot. You won't believe how many times. Think of all the money I would have made if the putt had gone in. I would have been, maybe, the captain of the Ryder Cup, a member of the Hall of Fame, a golf course designer. It would have been worth millions and millions, but that's life. You have to keep thinking of the good things."

COLOR HIS WORLD: "The color was part of me, part of my personality. At one point, I had 359 pairs of shoes. I have one of the most unbelievable closets you've ever seen. I've given a lot of the shoes away to Hall of Fames and to galleries. I used to get calls from people offering me hundreds of dollars, 'Doug, can you tell me what you're going to wear the next two days? We've got bets.'"

HAPPY DAYS: "We were a family. Everybody knew the wives' names, the kids' birthdays. Some of us didn't have a car, so we'd hitch a ride from tournament to tournament, and that made you closer. We'd go from Florida to California in maybe six carloads. The girls would get some sandwiches. We'd get a couple of cases of beer and sit around a motel pool to break up the trip."

8/26/03

Michael,

My best shot occured on my 51st birthday (11/13/94) during the season ending Tour Championship at The Dunes Club, Myrtle Beach S.C., where I set a (9 under par) course record 63

Bob Charles, Dave Stockton and I were playing the 15th hole, a par 5. After hitting a huge tee shot, I was faced with the decision of going for the green in two; for the very first time. It was an uphill 220 yard shot, into the wind and over a bunker to a narrow green with trees on both sides. I selected a 5 wood and hit it perfectly. I was hoping it would carry the bunker and when I saw the fans clap their hands I didn't think it enough to warrant the true results. As I walked up to join my playing partner, Dave asked me how many double eagles I had previously. I thought he was joking so I calmly told him I actually had 2 others and continued a few more steps until I actually realized that my 5 wood was in the hole for a 2.

Sincerely,
Jay Sigel

Jay Sigel

Jay Sigel spent the first stage of his golfing career playing for pride and country, winning back-to-back U.S. Amateurs in 1982 and 1983 and participating in nine Walker Cups. In 1994, the 50-year-old Sigel entered a second stage—the Champions Tour. He has been successful again, winning eight tournaments. Sigel, 60, also maintains an insurance business in Pennsylvania.

DEALT A DIFFERENT HAND: "I had a hand injury at Wake Forest, which led me in a different direction. I was in summer school, having finished exams, getting ready to go home. I was heading out to play golf with Coach Haddock. I went upstairs to make a phone call while he waited downstairs. I went through the dormitory door at the end of the hallway. The top half was window panes, the bottom half wooden. The door swung open. I put my hand up to stop it, but missed the paneling on the edge. My hand went through the window pane. It was a mess, and I still have damage today. It was a blessing. I wouldn't trade my amateur career for anything. All the people I met, all the Opens, the Masters, the Walker Cups, playing captain of the Walker Cup, the victories, I would have never experienced that."

DOUGH IS DEAR: "Judging one's results by the dollar signs was a very difficult thing. I was trying not to do it, but out here [on the Champions Tour] that's the way it has to be done. I had to act like money didn't mean anything when, in fact, it meant a lot. I had no exempt status. The Top 30 at the end of the year is determined by money."

JUST LIKE A GOOD NEIGHBOR: "I built a pretty nice business, and it's actually grown since I've played professionally. We do everything, primarily commercial, property and casualty, benefits, retirement planning, and life insurance. One of the problems I had out here was that I had 24 hours to work on my game, and I overdid it some. You have to have a balance."

Scott Simpson

Dear Ron,

You were asking about greatest shots we have ever hit, and what mine would be. Like most of us who have played for many years I do have some favorites. One that was probably most timely for me was my bunker shot on the 17th hole at the Olympic Club during the 1987 U.S. Open. I had just birdied 3 holes in a row and knew that I had a one shot lead on Tom Watson with no one else even close. He was the home town hero as a Stanford alumni, and had 8 major championships to my 0. I pulled my second shot just a little with my 4 iron and it caught the left bunker with the pin tucked on the front right of the green. I had quite a bit of green, but it was running away from me and pretty hard and fast. I was definitely nervous, but I picked my spot and stayed committed to hitting the shot like I practiced it. I hit through it well, it came out right where I wanted, and rolled down about 7 feet past the hole. I made the putt for par and was fortunate when it stood up for the one shot win.

Of all the great shots I have seen, I think Jack Nicklaus' one iron into the 17th at Pebble Beach to win the U.S. Open would be the one that stands out to me. He laced it into the wind, and it landed just short of the hole, hit the pin and stopped about 6 inches away. When you know how small and narrow that green is and in that situation it is just amazing. I would put Tom Watson's chip in on the same hole out of the rough to beat Nicklaus as a close second.

Best of luck with your book.

Sincerely,

Scott Simpson

Scott Simpson

Scott Simpson, 48, has won seven tour events, most notably the 1987 U.S. Open at The Olympic Club in San Francisco, edging Tom Watson by one stroke. A two-time All-American, he roomed at the University of Southern California with Craig Stadler in the late 1970s. Simpson, who plays with comedian Bill Murray each year at the Pebble Beach National Pro-Am, broke a five-year winless drought at the 1998 Buick Invitational before a hometown crowd in San Diego.

MY ROOMIE, THE WALRUS: "Craig was a good cook, though I'm not sure we always washed our pots and pans very well. Craig's dad actually got us a driving range net that he put up, so we could hit balls in our dining room. Of course, after a few beers, there would be a lot of windows missing. We ended renting a house that was condemned after we left. It was a wild neighborhood. Was Craig a slob? Overall, yes, but not always. Every once in a while, he would clean everything up."

ME AND BILL: "I wrote the tournament one year and asked if I could play with him. I didn't hear anything back until about two weeks before the next year. They said, 'You still want to play with him?' I said yes. We played that first year, in 1993, and had a great time, and that's when he pulled the lady in the bunker. We hit it off. We're good buddies. He's such a great guy. He's probably a little more serious than people think, and, contrary to what my kids think, maybe I'm funnier."

CALIFORNIA DREAMIN': "My kids will always remember the 1998 victory. My dad was there, the first time he saw me win in person. Stan Humphries [the former San Diego Chargers quarterback] caddied for me. I was struggling, not putting very well the first two days. It was only a three-round tournament because of the rain. I just putted great the last day and shot a 64. I birdied the last hole, but I still didn't think that would be good enough. I waited around, but nobody could do anything."

Dear Michael:

I'll never forget my greatest (favorite!) shot. It couldn't have come at a more appropriate time or place. The shot occurred during the 1985 B.C. Open at En-Joie golf course in Endicott, New York (my home town event). It seemed like everyone I knew was there cheering for the local boy!

In the final round, when I arrived at the 14th hole, a two hundred-ten yard par three, I saw Mike Reid make a bogey on the hole. The good news was that I was tied for the lead; but the bad news was that I still had to play the hole. With the pin front right, and some gnarly rough around the green, my plan was to aim slightly to the left and try to slide the ball in. If it didn't fade that would be okay, I still would have a putt for the lead. The five iron shot came off just like I imagined. It started just left of the flag and dropped to the right. After a soft bounce, and a few feet of roll, the ball went into the cup - just like a putt!!

The crowd went crazy (though many confessed that with all of the port-o-johns they actually missed the shot!!). I was in shock! I'm not a hat throwing kind of guy, so I high fived John, my longtime caddie, and simply walked down the fairway, soaked in the applause, and took the ball out of the cup. I didn't know what else to do! From that point on, I went into "protection" mode and won by a shot over Reid.

Making a hole in one is a big enough deal, but to actually get it on a hole that mattered AND near my hometown, in front of my family and friends, well, nothing could beat that!!

Sincerely,

Joey Sindelar

Joey Sindelar

Joey Sindelar has kept his card—and his cool—since arriving on the PGA Tour in the mid-1980s. Sindelar, 46, a three-time All-American at Ohio State and member of the school's 1979 national championship squad, has recorded six victories and pocketed more than $7 million. Sindelar's finest year came in 1988 when he won two tournaments (the Honda Classic and The International) and finished third on the money list.

GO NORTH, YOUNG MAN: "By playing golf in the late fall and early spring, you learn it's not the same as it is in the middle of the summer. The seven iron won't go 170. It may only go 145 if it's into the wind and 45 degrees and raining. These are great lessons to carry forward. You may not like it when you're doing it, but when you're done, you know it's been worth the test. Having a layoff in November and December does a lot for me. It's a great time to let your body heel, and, especially, to get your brain refreshed."

BEHAVE OURSELVES: "Our behavior is generally good on the course, though there are times when it could certainly be better. The tour has told us to police ourselves, which is fine, except I've gotten a few disappointing answers that way. One player told me, 'I've got to do what I've got to do.' Well, if Raymond Floyd had given me a lecture, that's not how I would have responded. I probably would've thrown up from fear. As competitive as we are, we have to be careful. It's tougher to be quiet when it hurts than yell when it hurts, but that's what we have to do. My biggest fear is dragging down my playing partner because he is out there trying to pay for his kid's college just like I am."

MIKE AND ME: "I grew up playing a lot of golf with Mike Hulbert. One of my fondest memories is when I'd go with my dad to hit balls off the second tee of a nearby public course. Mike would be out there, about 240 yards away, catching as many balls as he could with a first baseman's glove. He'd get mad at me if I weren't having a good day because he would have to run so much farther."

VIJAY SINGH

August 27, 2003

Dear Dr. Cherney:

My best shot would be the four iron I hit to reach the green in two on the par-five 15th hole at Augusta National Golf Club in the 2000 Masters Tournament.   The 15th is, of course, the hole made famous by Gene Sarazen's double eagle with a fairway wood, "the shot heard 'round the world" when he won the 1935 Masters.   In the years since then, many championships have also been lost there with wayward shots under the pressure of the final round, even though it has gone from a wood a mid-iron shot for the modern golfer.

Ahead of me that afternoon, Ernie Els had just birdied the 15th to pull within two strokes of my lead.   I needed a birdie there, but a shot into the water could possibly cost me the championship, as it did in 1985 to Curtis Strange and to others over the history of the Masters.   I had to block those thoughts out of my mind, and hit as pure a shot as I could, and I did, with the ball finishing within 20 feet of the hole.   From there, I took two putts for the birdie and an eventual three-stroke victory.

The next year, when I went back to the same spot, I was just in awe.   How did I ever pull that shot off?   I guess when you are in the thick of things, you don't always see the negatives, you only see the positives.

Sincerely,

Vijay Singh

Vijay Singh

In 2003, Vijay Singh, 41, accomplished what no professional golfer had been able to pull off since David Duval in 1998: He dethroned Tiger Woods from the top of the PGA Tour money list, earning more than $7.5 million. Singh, with four victories, moved up to No. 2 in the world rankings, posting eleven Top 10s in his final 12 appearances. Nobody spends more time on the driving range.

Since 1995, Singh has been a frequent contender in the tour's marquee events—the four majors, the Players Championship, and the season-ending Tour Championship. On three occasions, he came out on top:

1998 PGA CHAMPIONSHIP: At Sahalee Country Club in Washington, Singh prevailed by two strokes over Steve Stricker. Singh was ahead by only one when both players reached the 215-yard, par-3 17th hole. Singh converted a 15-footer for par, while Stricker was unable to make his 12-foot par attempt. Game, set, and match.

2000 MASTERS: Singh held off Duval, Woods, and Ernie Els to earn the green jacket. Singh arrived at the course early Sunday to complete his third round, converting two critical par putts to preserve a three-stroke advantage over Duval. However, after a bogey at 11 in the final round, Singh was up by just one. With 13 and 15 coming up, anything could happen.

Anything did—to Duval, whose second shot at 13 found Rae's Creek, leading to a bogey. Singh, meanwhile, saved par with a magnificent bunker shot at 12, and was steady the rest of the way.

2002 TOUR CHAMPIONSHIP: At East Lake Golf Club in Atlanta, Singh finally got even. Twice before, in 1998 and 2000, he had been in excellent position at East Lake to win the Tour Championship. Twice before, he came up short.

Not this time. Thanks to birdies on 9, 10, and 11, Singh regained control, assuming a four-stroke lead. A birdie at 17 by Charles Howell III narrowed the deficit but Singh parred 18 for the victory.

J.C. Snead
Hot Springs, Virginia

My Greatest Shot

It was at the T.P.C. in Dearborn, Michigan in 1995, The Ford Players Championship. It's Sunday, I'm on the 18th hole tied with Jack Nicklaus for the win. I'd been in the same position the year before and had blown it on this the final hole. As I prepared to tee off, I looked at my caddy Brian and said, "I might as well knock the hell out of it." I had a right center drive and was left with 187 yards to the pin. The pin placement was on the left and behind it was a TV tower about 25 feet right of the pin. I decided to aim for that tower and lo and behold, I hit exactly where I said I would hit it. I looked at Brian and said, "Hell, if I'd known it was gonna be that good, I would have just gone at the pin." I two putted to save par but remained tied with Nicklaus.

Now it was a playoff and we returned to the 18th once again. As Nicklaus and I prepared to tee off, I looked over at Jack and said, "OK Big Boy, let's get it on." Jack laughed and set up to tee off. My drive was probably only one to two feet from my first drive and I out-drove Jack by 10 to 15 yards. Jack hit first with a 4 iron to the middle of the green.

I looked at Brian and said "well, I know what club to hit but this time I'm going right at the pin." So with my 5 iron in hand, I aimed for the pin and what would become my greatest shot. I landed 3 ½ from the hole. Jack 2-putted and I made my putt for the birdie and the win.

J. C. Snead

Jesse Carlyle Snead had a tough act to follow. His uncle, Sam, was one of the game's all-time greats. But J.C. coped with the challenge quite well, winning eight tournaments on the PGA Tour, and four more on the Champions Tour. In 1987, he upset Seve Ballesteros in a playoff at Westchester Country Club. Snead, 63, spent four years in the Washington Senators farm system.

I AM NOT SAM: "How was I going to compete with him? I didn't start playing golf until I was 24 years old. It never entered my mind about competing with what he did. Nobody else has. I was proud to be his nephew, and we had a very good relationship. He was almost like a second father. I was proud of what he accomplished."

I AM NOT TED WILLIAMS: "I could run fast enough and had a good enough arm and hit good at times. Then, all of a sudden, I couldn't hit anything. It was time to move on. My other uncle, Pete, gave me a [golf] lesson and showed me how to use my hands. Instead of a great big slice, I started hitting a couple pretty straight, and it was kind of fun. I'm probably one of the few guys who have been on the tour and had a perfect amateur record. I never played an amateur event!"

OUTFOXING THE FOX: "At Westchester, Seve and I went to the 10th, a real short hole, about 315, 320 yards. I got up on the tee and told my caddie, 'Give me the driver.' I started swinging it real hard like I was going to try to drive the green. I could drive the green, but it was real risky. He [Seve] looked at me and went right over to get his driver out. It looked like his face was drawn. I told my caddie, 'It looks like he's choking worse than I am.' It kind of relaxed me. He hit that driver, a big pull hook. That ball hadn't gone 30 yards, I had a four-iron out. I hit it 100 yards from the green. I don't think he ever finished the hole."

SAM SNEAD

One of the best shots I ever hit was during the 1950 L.A. Open at Riviera Country Club. I needed a birdie on the last hole to win. The 18th hole turns to the right about half way up the fairway, and Sunday's pin is usually tucked behind the right-hand bunker. I had a strong wind in my face off the tee and needed to hit my tee shot up the left-hand side so that I could have a chance to go for the pin. I hit a low ball into the wind up the left, but when the ball landed it kicked dead right and backwards. I could barely see the green due to some overhanging tree limbs in the right rough area. I took out my one iron and hit a high cut shot up the left side and faded it onto the green. It landed like a butterfly with sore feet about nine feet from the hole. I made the putt to win the tournament for the second time.

Sam Snead

Sam Snead

Ask the experts who possessed the greatest golf swing ever, and the responses will be almost unanimous: "Slammin' Sammy" Snead. Born in Hot Springs, Virginia, Snead won a record 82 tournaments, 11 in 1950. Even way past his prime, he was still a threat, capturing the 1965 Greensboro Open for the eighth time at the age of 52. The only major prize to elude him was the U.S. Open. Snead passed away in 2002.

IF HE ONLY HAD A BRAIN: "He had the most natural talent of any golfer but had no golf brain. Hogan said that if Snead had a golf brain, we would all be playing for second. I was a really good friend of Snead's, but he was so tight with the buck. There was a 108-hole tournament in New York that Sam won where he pocketed $5,000. I finished last and won $25. We drove together to Chicago after the tournament and he never offered to pay for a meal or take care of the gas. We had to split everything down the middle."—*Johnny Bulla*

MAYBE HE DID HAVE ONE: "He capitalized on acting like he was a hillbilly, but he was smart. When you played Sam, you really had to play well if you were going to win. It was said that Sam turned so easily, the rhythm of his body, that he could swing in a telephone booth. I think that was somewhat true. He told stories, some of them good, some of them a little too dirty."—*Byron Nelson*

A GENIUS: "He was to the golf club like Michelangelo was with the brush. He was the best player I ever played with in my life. He was a very fun guy to be around. When Sam gambled with us, he would beat us out of $15 or $20, but if you got a four-hour playing lesson from Sam Snead for $20, that's pretty cheap."—*Chi Chi Rodriguez*

Jan Stephenson's Greatest Moments In Golf

My greatest shot/hole

In 1981 I was playing very well and my dad was on the bag. We had talked about how important sticking to my game plan was, and no matter what is happening with everyone else, I must stick to the plan. We were in Rochester and I was leading the tournament, but Lopez and Bradley were making a run at me. I was on the 17th which was a par 5, and I wanted to go for the green with my second shot. My dad said no and to stick to the game plan no matter what they were doing. I told him I was feeling good and I wanted to go for it. He reluctantly said okay and I missed it and ended up making bogey and placing 3rd. I promised him I would not do that again. The very next week at the Peter Jackson, the second major of the year (Canadian Open, now the British Open), I was leading and coming into 18. It was a par 5, and once again Lopez and Bradley was on my tail making another run. I was playing well and feeling good, I did not want to get into a playoff with either one of them and I told my dad I could get there in two. He told me no very sternly, and said you promised you would lay up. So I layed up, and I wasn't very happy about it. I had a sand wedge in about 75 yards, and I hit it to about 12 feet. The only problem, it was downhill with a left to right break (my worst putt), and heaps of spike marks all around the hole. I needed to make this putt to win. I was so nervous over the ball, I had to keep the putter head away from the ball because I was shaking so much I didn't want to hit the ball on accident. I thought to my self, do you have it in you to make this to win, and whatever you do don't run it by. I stood over it and let the putter go drained it to win my first major. My dad was crying, I was crying, and that was when I got the reputation for being a great putter.

My most memorable moment;

As a kid, my dad (Frank) would take me to the practice field to work on my game 3 times a day. We would go before school started, then in the afternoon once school was over, and one more time after dinner until dark. Dad loved working with me so much everyday, he took a night job with the Dept. of Transportation in order to make sure I was able to practice as much as I did. This was such a memorable time for me because I loved to practice, and because my dad was able to take me, it made practicing so much more enjoyable. The only thing about playing golf that I didn't like was having to play golf in bad weather. I couldn't stand the rain, and I really didn't like the cold. So one morning, when I was about 14 years old, the weather was freezing cold, and the last thing I wanted to do was practice. My dad came in to wake me to go and practice, and I told him I didn't feel like practicing, that it was too cold. He said "you have to practice, so get up and let's go". I didn't want to go, and we went back and forth for 20 minutes about me going to practice. Finally he got so cranky with me, he went to get my mum, and they both came into my room and said "if you practice today, you will win the U.S. Open someday". So I got up and went to practice. In 1983 after I won the U.S. Open in Tulsa, Oklahoma, my dad walked over to me from the gallery, as I was picking up the trophy and showing the world I had just won, my dad leaned over to me and said, "do you remember when I told you that you would win the U.S Open if you went to practice that day"? I leaned back over to him and said, "not only did I not forget, but that was the first thing I thought of when I made that putt to win, thanks dad and I love you".

Jan Stephenson

Jan Stephenson, another to make the long journey to America from Australia, has won 16 tournaments on the LPGA Tour. Her most significant accomplishment came in the 1983 U.S. Women's Open when she outlasted JoAnne Carner and Patty Sheehan by a shot. Stephenson was bold off the course, as well, posing as a model in the 1970s. In 2003, Stephenson, 52, teed it up against her male counterparts on the Champions Tour.

THE PINUP DAYS: "It's nice to not have that sex appeal anymore. I am 51 years old, after all! I never got paid. I just did it to help. Jane Blalock did not like sex selling golf, but she is now a good friend. We realize it is entertainment. Look at Tiger. Besides playing wonderfully, he also dresses great. I am an athlete first, but I try to be as feminine as possible. As far as my career, I might have won more if I was not bogged down with promoting the LPGA. That took a lot out of me mentally and physically during tournament week."

LIKE MICK JAGGER: "I didn't think that I would play past 30, then 35, then 40. But now I feel like I could play for 10 more years. I just love to compete. I am always trying to improve. I constantly ask Mark O'Meara and Tiger what they are working on and what's new. I still think my best golf is ahead of me. I am trying to help get a senior tour off the ground with Nancy Lopez, Beth Daniel, and JoAnne Carner. So I have the incentive to keep working at my game."

GOLF DOWN UNDER: "In America, teaching is more about marketing and public relations. You need a lot of money to be able to go to the big-name coaches. Golf is purer in Australia. Money is not necessary if you are good at a sport. The Institute of Sport will develop you. All the young Australian golfers have grown up through the Institute."

The greatest shot I ever hit was on the 18th hole at Riviera Country Club in the 1974 Glen Cambell L.A. Open.

As I stood on the 18th tee with a one shot lead on my playing partner Sam Snead, he approached me and said "You probably don't remember this but in the early 50's I birdied the last two holes to beat Ben Hogan here." I proceeded to hit my drive on the left hill leaving myself a 243-yard shot to the hole. The ball was 6 inches below my feet and I was into about a 15 mph wind. My options were limited as there was a steep hill left of the green, a drop off to the right and a cross bunker I had to carry at 190 yards.

Then with Sam standing beside my caddie, 50 yards from his own ball, I proceeded to hit the greatest 3 wood of my entire life. The ball finished 12 feet right of the hole and as I walked past Sam I said, "I guess Hogan didn't hit it that close." One putt later I had a 2 shot victory.

Regards,

Dave Stockton

P.S. In 20 times since, I've never even hit the green again from that spot.

Dave Stockton

Dave Stockton has excelled at every level of professional golf. He won 11 events on the PGA Tour, including two PGA Championships (1970, 1976). In 1991, as captain, he anchored the United States to a dramatic Ryder Cup victory at Kiawah Island. On the Champions Tour, Stockton, 62, has prevailed on 14 occasions, including the 1996 U.S. Senior Open.

THE WAR BY THE SHORE: "The highlight to me of the '91 Ryder Cup was either Tuesday or Wednesday night when we had the teams with their families at a cookout. To me, that's what it was all about. I remember finding out that Bernhard Langer's daughter, who was around two and a half, might have a terminal illness. Five days later, the match came down to his putt on the final green. For the United States, I wanted him not to make it. But, for him and how small the sport is that we play compared to life, I was hoping he would make it. She turned out okay."

TWO PGAS ARE BETTER THAN ONE: "The first, when I had to go head-to-head against Palmer, I won that one. Nobody gave it to me. I just destroyed the field. The second victory at Congressional, which turned out to be my last win on tour, totally satisfied me that I wasn't in the league with those who had won only one major championship. I won two majors. Two puts you in a different class."

A-HUNTING WE WILL GO: "It frees me up, letting me relax. A successful hunt is not the kill. A successful hunt is no phones, maybe meeting new friends. My dad owned a sporting goods store, so I used to hunt and fish. I started out by carrying sticks and got the privilege of helping find the birds after they were shot. When I got big enough, I carried the birds, and then I was able to carry an unloaded gun. It was a slow process. Finally, I got to shoot. My most enjoyable hunt was in British Columbia, 95 miles from the nearest road. I saw the Northern Lights. I was out there on my own, and it was just phenomenal."

Curtis Strange

In the late 1980s, nobody in professional golf played at a higher level than Curtis Strange, who captured back-to-back U.S Opens at The Country Club and Oak Hill, the first player to accomplish the feat since the legendary Ben Hogan (1950, 1951). Strange recorded 17 victories overall and won three money titles in a four-year period. Strange, 49, the U.S. captain in the 2002 Ryder Cup, works as the lead analyst for ABC.

GOING FOR THE TRIFECTA: "I gave myself a chance, not only during the week but leading up to it. I thought I could do it. I remember the third [U.S. Open] as much as the other two because it was all part of that time in my life that was special. Maybe [in succeeding years] I expected too much out of myself every day I walked out on the golf course, and that led to trouble because I started messing with my swing. It's the years after the Open victories that I'm not proud of, as far as my golf. But that's the way this game is."

DAILY DOUBLE: "[Having a twin, Allen] is the only thing I've ever known. I don't know what it would be like not to be a twin. I was fortunate to have someone around to compete with every minute of every day, not only to play golf; we both were athletes in other sports. There was always someone to throw the baseball with, someone to hit balls with. It was a big part of the equation to have someone who could beat you every time you turned around."

READY FOR ACT II: The number one game in town is the PGA Tour, but to compete against the guys you competed against before will be exciting. I think everything I'm doing now is gearing for the seniors, as far as health issues go and my game. If I play, I want to give myself a chance. I know what it's like to play 12 events, and my game can't exist on 12 events."

10-22-00

Dear Sir,

Good shots become great ones when magnified by the pressure of the tournament or situation. Professionals hit perfect shots every day, but can they do the same for their dream to come true.

I was fortunate enough to do just that in 1988 U.S. Open. On the 72nd hole, my 3rd shot, a simple bunker shot, landed 18 inches from the hole to send me to a playoff vs. Nick Faldo.

I went on to win the next day, but if it wasn't for the simple bunker shot,

Curtis Strange
Captain

SEPTEMBER 25-30, 2001

CURTIS STRANGE
Captain

my dream would not have ever come true. It was the most important shot of my life.

Thank you,

Curtis Strange

Louise Suggs

LPGA Founder
LPGA Tour Hall of Fame member
LPGA Teaching and Club Professional Hall of Fame member

One of the best shots I remember hitting was at the 1948 Ladies British Amateur Championship at Royal Lytham & St. Annes Golf Club. I was on the front nine of the morning round of the finals competing against Jean Donald from Gullane, Scotland. We played a 36-hole final round. We were on a par 4 with strong cross winds. My caddie told me to aim about 25-30 yards right of the green. I did just that and remarkably the wind brought it back and the ball ran into the cup for a two. It was just one of those shots you really didn't expect to work as well as it did. That was so much fun to see. Jean had out driven me on this hole and everyone thought she had her putt to halve the hole with me. And, she nearly holed it, but didn't, and I ended up winning the match which went all 36 holes.

Lew Worsham's shot at the Tam O'Shanter event in the early 1950s was one of the best shots I've ever seen. He was on the 72nd hole of play and he needed a birdie to tie. I happened to be playing in the group ahead of Lew and had the opportunity to watch him finish the hole. He was playing the short par-4 with a pitching wedge to the green. He appeared to hit it thin, but it hit the front of the green and as the announcers and Jimmy Demaret were offering play-by-play of the action, Lew's shot rolled right on up to the hole and went in the cup. It was marvelous to watch the ball work its way into the cup. We all know he could make a three to tie, but it was marvelous to see him make a two for the win.

Louise Suggs

Louise Suggs

Louise Suggs claimed the top prize 58 times in her storied career and finished in the Top 10 on the money list every season from 1950 through 1961. At the 1949 U.S. Women's Open in Maryland, she won by an unprecedented 14 strokes over Babe Zaharias, one of 11 major victories. One of the LPGA's 13 founders, Suggs, nicknamed "Miss Sluggs," by Bob Hope, was inducted to the LPGA Tour Hall of Fame in 1967.

FROM THE GROUND UP: "It was hard in the early days because we had to travel everywhere by car. But there was no animosity. We were happy to be able to have a little money to play for, and it was more like a sorority than a dog-eat-dog thing. I made some lasting friendships. I don't know if I'd be interested in trying again, but I'm glad it happened. We were so dumb, we didn't know it didn't have a good chance. In those days, women in golf were persona non grata. Nobody could figure out why we were even trying to play for money. When I go down today and see the LPGA's office building, I think to myself, Dear God, this is what we started. And here it is!"

THE MUSICAL BABE: "Babe Zaharias was not only talented as an athlete, but was a fine musician with a lovely voice. We had get-togethers at night somewhere, and somebody would always have a guitar. She played the harmonica. It was good, fun stuff, no drinking in those days. At night, there wasn't too much to do. We were in small towns, mostly."

THANKS FOR THE NICKNAME: "First time I ever saw Bob Hope, when I was 17 years old, I was so excited. This was during an exhibition match with Bing Crosby and Johnny Weissmuller. I hit one of those shots that was just unreal. It must have gone 275 yards, or something like that. He started to walk off the tee. Bing yelled at him, 'Where do you think you're going?' And Hope said, 'I'm going to get a skirt. I'm not going to play with that Sluggs.'"

Carol Semple Thompson

March 18, 2003

Dear Ron,

In response to your inquiry about great golf shots that I have hit, there are two 5-iron shots that keep floating around in my brain. In 1973 during the 36-hole final of the U.S. Women's Amateur I had just gone 3 down to Anne Sander on about the 24th hole. The next hole was a par three where I succeeded in hitting a truly pure 5 iron that ended up 1 inch behind the hole. That birdie gave me a big lift and put me back in the match. Eventually I won the match 1 up on the 36th hole for my first national championship.

On the other hand, in 1994 during the first round of the U.S. Women's Open I managed to skull a 5 iron into the hole on the 15th hole for an eagle and went on to shoot 66 and lead the Open for a few hours before Helen Alfredsson came in with a 63. The moral must be that it absolutely does not matter one bit how the ball gets into the hole.

More recently, I had the wonderful opportunity to compete this past summer in my 12th Curtis Cup Match at Fox Chapel Golf Club in Pittsburgh, my home town. The U.S. had a substantial lead going into the second afternoon singles and needed only one point to tie and keep the Cup in the U.S. Unfortunately, the tide turned during that round and we found ourselves behind in too many matches. I was playing in the second position and, after a poor start, I had managed to pull even and then go one up on the seventeenth hole. On the eighteenth my opponent was on the green below the hole with a reasonable birdie putt. My birdie putt on the other hand was 27 feet long, downhill and breaking. As I hit my putt I knew it was going to be close, but it took forever to creep downhill and finally on its last gasp drop in the hole. It was absolutely a storybook finish to win my match and be instrumental in winning the Curtis Cup in front of so many friends and family.

As far as amazing shots I have observed, that would go to Jose Maria Olazabal in the 1999 Masters. I was an off duty rules official spectating on the 13th hole the final day. Mr. Olazabal hit his drive in a precarious position on pine straw in the right trees not 20 feet from where I was standing. He proceeded to pull 5 or 6 pine needles from under and around his ball. Each time he pulled a needle away in slow motion I died a thousand deaths knowing that if his ball moved he would incur a stroke penalty and I would be obligated to call that penalty. How his ball stayed in place I will never know. At any rate he hit a magnificent iron on the green and went on to birdie the hole. A higher power was watching over him that that day.

Your project sounds like great fun. I wish you well in getting all of these letters published. I will look forward to the final product.

All the best,

Carol

Carol Semple Thompson

Few players in the history of amateur golf have achieved as much as Carol Semple Thompson. Thompson, from the small town of Sewickley, Pennsylvania, has made a record 12 Curtis Cup appearances, posting 18 victories. In 1973, she captured the U.S. Amateur. A year later, she won the British Ladies Open Amateur. In 2003, Thompson, 55, made it to the semifinals of the U.S. Women's Senior Amateur.

NO ON PRO: "I thought about it when I first graduated from college in 1970, but there wasn't a lot of money on the women's tour, and my parents didn't want me to turn pro. My father offered to support me for a year if I didn't. I figured any red-blooded American college graduate who didn't take him up on that offer would be crazy. I went to Florida and played all winter. The following summer, I was really discouraged with my golf and didn't want to turn pro. I put it off and then two years later I won the U.S. Women's Amateur. I loved that. I let the chance to turn professional go by, and I'm really glad. I've been so successful as an amateur. I would have been just another touring professional."

LET'S PLAY TWO!: "First of all, I didn't expect I would ever win the U.S. Amateur, and when I did, and then won the British, it was surreal. Winning the U.S. was very much for my parents, because my mother was really sick at the time and my father was vice president of the USGA. When I won the British, that was more for me."

FOX HUNTING: "I've grown up fox hunting. I get on a horse and follow the hounds, which are following a scent that has been dragged through the woods. It used to be that people thought foxes were terrible things because they killed all their chickens and piglets, but now it's just become more sport. It's wonderful to see the hounds scent their way around the countryside. The rush of it is that I'm fearing for my life as I go galloping across and go over these jumps."

ESTEBAN TOLEDO

Dear Michael:

On the last hole of the 1997 Tour Qualifying School in Grenelefe, Florida, I was in real trouble. I needed a birdie to get my card, my playing privileges for a whole year. But things sure didn't look good. I was lying three on the par 5, and I still wasn't even on the green, about 20 feet short of the pin. My only chance was to sink a very difficult downhill chip with my 60 degree wedge.

I was so nervous, I backed off. I backed off a second time and then a third time. I just couldn't hold my club, and my legs were shaking. John, my father, who was my caddie, my sponsor, and my cheerleader, told me: 'Just take a deep breath and swing at it.' Finally, I did, and I feared right away that I missed it. I was sure that I had hit it too far, too fast, and didn't get the loft that I needed for the ball to slowly make its way toward the cup. Goodbye PGA Tour.

Just then, remarkably, the ball started curving to the left, and checking up. With each revolution, it looked better and better. All of a sudden, it disappeared. The first thing I did was look up into the sky. 'Thank you, Lord, for that,' I said. Because, surely, that wasn't me who made that pitch. That was God. I hugged my dad and started to cry. I knew what making that chip meant. I had made it to the Tour once before, in 1994, but didn't do well enough to stick around. This time, I would stick around. Now I'm out here making a lot of money.

On the way to the airport that night, we were so excited that we missed the exit. We turned around, and got to the plane just in time. I suppose one drama for the day wasn't enough.

I've played with Tiger and Greg Norman and made some great shots, but none ever mattered like the one at Tour school.

Sincerely,

Esteban Toledo

Esteban Toledo

Unlike many of his fellow professionals, Esteban Toledo didn't grow up in a world of privilege. He grew up in poverty. The youngest of 11 children, he fought his way out, literally, sporting a 12–1 record as a professional boxer. Toledo hasn't abandoned his roots, planning to build a church in Mexico. Toledo, 31, has played seven full seasons on the tour, pocketing more than $3 million.

IN THIS CORNER: "My brother, Mario, took me to the gym because I used to get beat up at school every single day for four or five months. I was 12 years old. I moved to the city, to a big school. Everybody was picking on the way I dressed, the way I talked. I never thought I would be a boxer. I did it to get my revenge. Boxing and golf have nothing in common. But the discipline you use for boxing, that's what I use for golf, the determination, the dedication."

SING FOR YOUR SUPPER: "I didn't have what a lot of people had. I used to be very hungry every night. I used to go to the corner and take a bus all the way to downtown. I would sing songs to get money so I could eat. I made enough to go to the store and get a meal. It was embarrassing. I got in trouble many times. Once, I stole a little toy car and got caught. The owner of the house asked why I stole the car. I told him because I never had one before. The guy let me go, realizing I meant what I said, and gave me the toy. I went home and played with it."

GIVING BACK: "The barrio where I grew up, there is no church, and there are no morals. There is, basically, no education. I want someone to come over and teach those kids to go to school and become successful, and have dreams. Right now, they don't have it. I want them to stay away from drugs."

6/16/03

Dear Ron,

Please excuse the delay in answering your request. In December 1953, I was to play in the Havana Open and be married the following week to Lynn Stewart in Coral Gables, Florida. I had invited her to fly over to Havana and watch the final two rounds of play, and as she watched the final round in back of the 18th green, I was faced with a golf shot from the 17th fairway to the green that called for a slice that would curve some thirty to forty feet. I selected a four iron and started the ball between two Royal palms well left of the green. The shot landed on the green and rolled to rest about two feet from the hole! I made the putt for birdie to avoid a 5-way playoff for first place. We were married the following week and will have been married 50 years on December 14th, 2003.

Sincerely,

Bob Toski

For more than 30 years, Bob Toski has been recognized as one of the game's most prominent instructors, the co-founder of the Golf Digest schools and author of more than a dozen books. His students have included Chi Chi Rodriguez, Tom Kite, and Judy Rankin. In 1954, he was the leading money winner on the PGA Tour. Toski, 77, competed on the Champions Tour in the 1980s and early 1990s.

TIPS ON TEACHING: "It's really communication, to help the student realize that even though you may make the teaching of the swing simplistic, the timing and control of the human body relative to the force of the swing is difficult. You have to remember that the average student is not athletically endowed, like the tour player, and therefore gets confused easily. My advice for beginners is to take instruction from a teacher who understands and can communicate the fundamentals properly. Become an orthodox player, according to the basics: The grip, the stance, ball position, posture, pace. If you try to play golf without good instruction, you're not going to improve."

CLOSER TO HOME: "My wife and I had three children in 1955, 1956, and 1957. Coming from a large family, we were a product of our environment. I didn't want to play anymore [on tour] while my wife was home alone with the three kids. I got a club job, and when I became very proficient as a teacher, *Golf Digest* recognized my communication skills and my teaching abilities and hired me to become a member of their panel. That's how the golf schools started. I have no regrets. I became successful as a teacher, and I'm real proud of that. There have been very few players who became successful teachers—Tommy Armour, Paul Runyan, Claude Harmon."

BEFORE THEIR TIME: "In the modern generation, the younger players I teach today weren't even born when I played the tour. They only know me as a teacher. My longevity as a teacher has been greater than my longevity as a player. I only played on the tour for five or six years. I quit at the age of 30 to start teaching."

Mitch Voges

When Mitch Voges captured the 1991 U.S. Amateur, he became, at 41, the third oldest winner in the championship's history. A month later, Voges, who played at Brigham Young University with Johnny Miller, was a key member of the victorious U.S. Walker Cup squad. In recent years, Voges, 54, who has tried to qualify for the Champions Tour, has worked as a radio and television commentator.

MAKING THE GRADE: "Winning the Amateur answered a lot of questions I had about myself, not only as an athlete, but as a competitor. In the final, I had nine birdies and an eagle on the first 20 holes on a very difficult golf course [the Honors Course in Chattanooga, Tennessee]. I felt at peace with myself. At the end of the day, that was more important than worrying about external pressures."

BACK TO THE FUTURE: "I had two ruptured discs and a problem with the vertebrae in my lower back. My back got to the point where I couldn't function that much. I couldn't get a good pillow fight going with my son and I couldn't pick up my little girl walking around Disneyland. 'I give up,' I said. I had the thing fixed and was out of competitive play for about 10 years. I spent most of a year in a body brace without doing anything, without hitting a golf shot or a putt. In 1984, I started playing pretty good and went to qualify for the U.S. Mid-Amateur. I was the medalist. Walking up the 18th hole, a par 5, I cried all the way from the tee to the green. I thought to myself, 'It's not gone.'"

GAINING PERSPECTIVE: "I don't like playing that much where it consumes you. I don't like what it does to the guys who do that, and I don't like what it does to me when I do that. It's like when I was a kid and I saw people come on the Johnny Carson show. The first question was: How's your career going? It was all about me. That aspect of professional athletics has always bothered me. I got married when I was 19. I've always had a family. To me, the most important commitments I have are to my wife and my children."

MITCH VOGES
U.S. Amateur Champion

If you play competitive golf long enough you're bound to hit some shots that encompass the full spectrum from good to bad to ugly. In order to preserve a modicum of dignity, mention will be made here of one good shot and one that could have been ugly but turned out good.

Shortly after capturing the United States Amateur Championship at the Honors Course in 1991 I was selected to play on the U.S. Walker Cup team. As a 41 year old with a day job and precious little time to play competitive golf it was quite an honor. Members of the team included Phil Michelson, David Duval, Jay Sigel, and Allen Doyle. Most of the other members have all gone on to distinguish themselves in competitive play as well.

Our team traveled to Portmarnock, Ireland for the matches and it was an emotional week. I remember bursting into tears when I opened the boxes containing my bag and uniform emblazoned with United States of America and the USGA logo. At the flag raising ceremony I was introduced last by Captain Jimmy Gabrielson as "our American Champion." The memory still tugs at my heart today.

The first day of matches went as we had hoped. Our side jumped into a formidable lead and the final day appeared to be pretty much ceremonial. We had a strong team and were all playing with a great deal of confidence. At the team meeting the night before the last day's play we all had a chance to express our feelings. Captain Gabrielsen announced the line-up and said he was sending me out last in the clean-up position. It was a stunning honor given the quality of players in the room.

The next morning things took a turn for the worse. Those who know say the galleries were the largest in Walker Cup history and unquestionably partisan as you would expect. As far as we were concerned silence from the crowd was golden. It was the roars for GB&I players that stung. Our side got dusted in the morning foursomes and the gallery sensed a comeback. GB&I held the Cup having won it two years prior at Peach Tree in Atlanta and didn't want to let go.

When the final singles matches began things were tense. As he had all week, Phil Michelson led off and jumped into a good lead in his match. Few of those who followed had similar luck. It's hard to play when you can't breathe and your hands are shakey. Roars erupted from all over the course the final afternoon and the aura was intimidating.

I was playing well but not able to win a hole from my opponent and when I drove into a blind pot bunker 330 yards down the 9th fairway I lost the hole and turned one down. It was becoming apparent the outcome would hinge on the last two matches. As we made the turn I caught Bobby May walking off the 10th tee in the group ahead and gave him my assessment. I'd known Bobby since he was 14 and told him to take care of his man (he was even) and I'd get my guy. We exchanged determined glances and went to work.

Bobby forged ahead in his match and I won the 10th to square mine. On the long par four 11th hole my opponent and I both hit big drives with mine about 5 yards further. The entire fairway and green was lined with spectators and when he unleashed a long iron to the back of the green the roar was intense. The flag was cut front right just over a bunker with a severe slope just right of the green. The wind was blowing about 15 mph from the right off the Irish Sea.

From 190 yards I hit my best "butter cut" 4 iron to hold the flight against the wind. It looked good all the way but when the ball disappeared over the corned of the bunker there was dead silence! I checked with my caddie about the outcome and he said "your stoney mate" meaning it was close. There was zero reaction from the gallery.

I jumped and bobbed all the way up the fairway straining to get a fix on the ball with the hope it had not run through the corner of the green and down the slope into a difficult position. As I got about 100 yards from the green there was a lone voice that still brings tears to my eyes. It was my wife as she yelled "great shot Mitch," which was immediately followed by polite but subdued applause. Then came a few more encouraging shouts from USGA officials in blue blazers. The ball was 3' right of the cup!

The contrast in the responses from my opponent's shot and mine really got me fired up. As is, I went on to birdie 3 of the next 5 holes and clinched the victory. The memory of having the USGA officials run to hug me when it was over will never fade. But it pales in comparison to the lone female voice from the 11th fairway when my game and heart were facing the sternest test an amateur golfer can experience. Our's was the first team to take the Walker Cup off foreign soil when it was held overseas.

On a lighter note, while approaching the 18th green at Pebble Beach, during the first round of the '92 U.S. Open I discovered that my son, Christian, who was caddying for me, had left the putter against a water cooler, back at the tee---540 yards away.

Christian had run cross country in high school and I briefly thought about having him high tail it back to the tee. But I came to my senses and realized he couldn't run 3 quarters of a mile before it would be my turn to putt. Payne Stewart was at the back of the green and Ian Baker Finch faced a short pitch.

Looking back down the fairway David Duval was waiving my putter high in the air but it was time to get resourceful. On national television I knocked in a curling fifteen footer...with my three wood! Christian got a "take-a-hike" from a sports anchor and I got Golf Digest's "Putt of the Year".

Your Friend,

Mitch Voges

Mitch Voges

DUFFY WALDORF

Dear Michael:

For my best shot, the choice is obvious: Final hole, final round of the 1999 Buick Classic at Westchester Country Club just outside New York City. My second shot to the par 5 landed in the bunker in front of the green, about 30 yards short of the pin tucked in the back.

To get into a playoff with Dennis Paulson, I needed to get up and down. Much easier said than done. I was not, to be honest, renowned for my bunker game, and it wasn't the type of shot I had played in a long time, even practiced. There was no option of running it up, either. I had to carry the ball to the upper plateau. The odds were not good.

Typically, with that kind of shot, you leave the ball short. So I told myself: 'Swing hard enough to think that you're going to hit it into the crowd behind the green.' I swung hard and caught it just right, leaving myself a five-foot putt for the birdie. If I had been in the fairway, and had a square blade, that shot would probably have gone 60 or 70 yards. I made the putt and won the tournament with another birdie on the first playoff hole.

The victory meant the world to me, my first in four long years. People say the first win is the hardest. Maybe so, but the second win ain't easy, either. Coming through at Westchester started me on a little run. I won two more tournaments in the next 18 months. Heading into that week, I was on pace to lose my card. I had already lost a lot of my confidence. But pulling off one of the hardest shots in the game turned everything around.

Sincerely,

Duffy Waldorf

Duffy Waldorf

With an assortment of zany hats and shirts, Duffy Waldorf has been one of the tour's most distinctive characters since he arrived on the scene in the late 1980s. Each week, he uses golf balls with messages and reminders from his family. A star at UCLA, Waldorf, 41, has won four times and has often placed in the Top 90 on the money list. In both 1999 and 2000, he won more than $1.3 million.

HATS OFF TO HIM: "I was sponsored by a local course, where we were allowed to buy clothes and hats. They had this one hat that was Hawaiian style with pink flowers and the Hawaiian print. When I got to Greensboro in 1991, I got tired of wearing my white hat. So I wore this Hawaiian hat on Friday and tied for the lead after two rounds. I wore it the rest of the time. The next week, I wore a white hat for a round or two, and everyone wanted to know where the Hawaiian hat was. It had gotten so much exposure on television. Ever since the Greensboro tournament, I've been wearing the flowered hat. I have 50 to 75 at home."

A NAME THAT STUCK: "I had the same name as my dad, James, so my grandmother and my mom wanted to find a nickname. I used to fall on my duff a lot. I got the name when I was only 18 months old, and I've been known as Duffy ever since. I've always liked it. It seemed like the right name to be called."

GUTTY BIG BRUINS: "I played with such great players in college: Corey Pavin, Tom Pernice Jr., Steve Pate, Jay Delsing. I redshirted a year and then played with Brandt Jobe and Scott McCarron. The number of tour players from my five years is pretty incredible. Eddie Merrins, our coach, was different from a lot of coaches. He delegated traveling responsibilities to the assistants and just worked with us on our games when we were home. We still occasionally work together at Bel-Air Country Club in Los Angeles."

E HARVIE WARD

The greatest shot I ever hit was in the first round of the US Amateur at the James River golf course in Richmond, Virginia in 1955. It was the ninth time I had played in the Amateur. The furthest I had made it prior to 1955 was the quarterfinals in 1947. Skee Riegel won it that year.

In 1955, I was playing Ray Palmer and was one down going into 18 which was a par 5 the USGA had turned into a par 4. We both hit identical drives. As we got closer to the balls, I could see that one was 6 inches in the rough and one was 6 inches in the fairway. I was lucky to have my ball be the one in the fairway and was able to knock it on the green, a shot well over 200 yards. Ray had to lay up, as there was a big cross-bunker down near the green. I won the hole to square the match. I was able to beat him on the 19th hole and go on to win the US Amateur that year. Those were the most important 6 inches of my golf career.

Hope this helps and thanks for thinking of me.

Regards,

E Harvie Ward

E. Harvie Ward

E. Harvie Ward, 77, seized back-to-back U.S. Amateur titles in 1955 and 1956. A year later, Ward almost became the first amateur to ever wear a green jacket, finishing fourth. Ward, who teamed up with his longtime friend, Ken Venturi, in a storybook match against Ben Hogan and Byron Nelson in 1956 at Cypress Point, became a top-notch instructor in North Carolina. One of his prize pupils was Payne Stewart.

THE MATCH: "At the time, it was just a match. I didn't think anything about it. Hogan pitched in on the 10th hole for an eagle, and that was the difference. Kenny and myself weren't afraid or in awe of Hogan and Nelson. We felt we could beat these guys. I had just won the Amateur, and Kenny was on the top of his game. We were playing two guys that were on the shady side of the mountain."

NO SURE THING: "All these boys in amateur golf are trying to do today is enhance their resume so they can turn pro. They play like pros because that's what they're shooting for. When I played, 90 to 95 percent could care less about pro golf, and that's why the good players remained amateurs. There was no money in it. I can't blame these players. The only thing I find wrong is that too many think they can play, but can't play at the professional level. I remember some amateurs who were great players, but never turned out to be anything. Making a living in pro golf is not a sure thing."

A NATURAL PAYNE: "I was more or less of a father image for him, as much as anything. His swing was so good. The one thing he fought was overswinging. When he overswung, he tended to be a little wild. You don't teach a guy like Payne or Freddy Couples about mechanics. You just have to be sure he's got enough gas in the car to get where he is going. We had a lot of fun together, on and off the course. His swing was so natural."

Tom Watson

During the late 1970s and early 1980s, Tom Watson was the best player in the world. Watson captured eight majors, including five British Opens, and was the leading money winner four years in a row (1977-1980). With 39 victories, Watson, 54, is tied for ninth on the all-time list. In 2003, he won two majors on the Champions Tour and brought back memories with a first-round 65 at the U.S. Open.

A LINKS CONVERT: "The links game did not fit in with my game at first. I had designed my game to hit the ball high, like Jack Nicklaus. I had a hard time hitting the ball low. I thought the game was played to carry the ball onto the green and stop it. Even though I won British Opens in 1975 and 1977, I did not particularly like the links-style game. It wasn't until 1979 that I really changed my attitude. I changed it very simply because I said, 'Why am I fighting this? Play the game like you did as a kid.'"

LORD BYRON: "Byron [Nelson] came to me in 1974 after I lost to Hale Irwin in the last round of the U.S. Open, shooting 79 at Winged Foot. He asked me that, if I ever needed some help, please give him a call. I took him up on that offer about a year and a half later. Following that, I had my watershed year, 1977. I went to visit him many times, staying at his ranch. I enjoyed being around a man who had such a wonderful understanding, not only of the game, but of the history two generations before me."

MAKING FRIENDS: "I watched my father and his friendships with his playing partners. The game of golf makes that happen. There's a certain understanding that golfers have about the game. It creates a brotherhood. The trials and tribulations of the game, the funny happenings, the different types of weather conditions—you all share the same thing. You understand what it is to have a bad bounce at the wrong time or a good bounce at the right time, or hit that perfect shot or miss that short putt."

TOM WATSON DESIGN 7/18

Dear Mr. Cherney,

In response to your questions the greatest shot I ever played was the short 16 ft. chip on the 71st hole (17th green) of the 1982 U.S. Open. Tied with Jack Nicklaus the chip in

put me one ahead with one to
play to be champion of our
National Open.

I birdied the final hole to
win by 2 shots, and received
the trophy of the championship I
had coveted the most.

Hope this helps. Sincerely,
Tom Watson

Mike Weir

AIR CANADA CHAMPIONSHIP 1999

I'VE BEEN DEBATING WHICH SHOT HAS BEEN MY OWN PERSONAL "GREATEST SHOT" AND I THINK IT HAS TO BE THE 8 IRON ON THE 14TH HOLE FINAL RD. OF THE AIR CANADA CHAMPIONSHIP.

THERE HADN'T BEEN A CANADIAN WIN IN CANADA IN OVER 50 YRS ON THE P.G.A TOUR AND AS I STOOD OVER MY 2ND SHOT ON 14 THAT WAS ABOUT TO CHANGE.

I WAS TIED FOR THE LEAD AND A LITTLE ANXIOUS ABOUT TRYING TO CAPTURE MY 1ST TOUR WIN. I HAD 164 YDS A LITTLE DOWNWIND AND I ACTUALLY VISUALIZED THE BALL GOING IN THE HOLE BEFORE I STRUCK THE SHOT. I SIMPLY ADDRESSED THE BALL AND TRUSTED MYSELF AND THE SHOT CAME OFF JUST AS I HAD SEEN IN MY MIND EARLIER AND I WAS A SURPRIZED AS ANYONE WHEN IT DISAPPEARED IN THE HOLE..

THE WHOLE SCENE WAS CRAZY AFTER THAT BUT I MANAGED TO REMAIN FOCUSED THE LAST 4 HOLES AND WIN MY FIRST P.G.A TOUR EVENT BY 2.

Mike Weir

Mike Weir, a hero in his homeland of Canada, captured the 2003 Masters, outdueling Len Mattiace on the first extra hole. Weir, a lefty, won three tournaments last season and was a strong candidate for Player of the Year honors. He's a three-time winner of the Lionel Conacher Award, given to his nation's top male athlete. Weir, 33, is the first Canadian to compete in the Presidents Cup.

DEAR JACK: "The one thing that was difficult when I was a kid was that there wasn't a lot of lefthanded equipment around. It may have helped me. I carried a three-, five-, seven-, and nine-iron and a driver. Because I didn't have a sand wedge, I hit little nine-irons out of the bunkers and had to create some more shots. I wrote a letter to Jack Nicklaus, asking him if I should switch to righthanded from lefthanded. I got a letter back, and it was pretty cool. He said no, that I should stick to my natural swing. I have it framed in my office."

FACE OFF: "I grew up playing hockey, a long time before I started playing golf. I love the sport and had ambitions to play professionally, but wasn't good enough. I like the team aspect of it, the physical contact, and I love the speed and the strategy. It's so different from golf. In golf, you kind of create the motion, while in hockey you react to the shots. The players come to hit you. It's such a high-energy game. Maybe I've transferred the competitive nature of hockey a little into my golf."

BE LIKE MIKE: "I don't see myself differently [since winning the Masters]. It was a win for me, my family, and all the people who have been committed to my game, but also a win for the fans in Canada who have been really supportive. When I was back there for a few charity events, I noticed that there were more kids out there playing. I know the game is getting more popular in Canada."

June 01, 2002

Dear Ron,

The best shot I ever saw was a shot by Mickey Wright. We were playing a course in French Lick, Indiana. The hole was a par four, dogleg left, slightly uphill. There was a tree in the middle of the fairway about 200 yards off the tee. Mickey hit the tree, and the ball fell just back and to the right. She was able to take a backswing, but the follow through was going to be restricted by the tree. I saw her taking a few practice swings with a full backswing, stopping the club just after impact. I couldn't believe what I was seeing so I moved closer to better observe. Sure enough, she took what looked like a five or four iron, took the backswing and came through and stopped the club before hitting the tree. The ball shot off up the hill onto the green. It was about a one hundred fifty or sixty yard shot. Mickey was truly a remarkable player.

I think one of the best shots I ever hit was in Sarasota, Florida, at Bent Tree Country Club. It was on the 18th hole, the final round of the tournament, and I was tied for the lead with Hollis Stacy. The hole was a par five, dogleg right, with water down the right side of the fairway. Hollis hit her tee shot into the water which left me a little breathing room. However, I knew Hollis was a competitor and would probably still par the hole. I managed to keep my drive in the fairway, and played a conservative second shot that left me with about one fifty or one sixty to the pin. The wind was blowing about 25mph that day. The way the green was designed, it would be a shorter shot to go to the front of the green, but that would leave about a 70 foot putt. So I decided to go for the pin. I hit a two iron onto the green about 15 feet from the pin. It was my best two iron shot ever, especially under the conditions. And as it turned out, that par was good enough to win.

Sincerely,

Kathy Whitworth

Kathy Whitworth

Nobody in the history of the game, man or woman, has collected more official tour victories than Texas native Kathy Whitworth, who finished her career with 88, six more than Sam Snead. Other accomplishments include: Player of the Year seven times, Vare Trophy (lowest stroke average) recipient seven times, and leading money winner eight times. Whitworth, 64, was elected into the LPGA Tour Hall of Fame in 1975.

OPEN AND CLOSED SHUT: "Everybody wants to win the U.S. Open, and my problem was that I wanted to win it too badly. I overreacted to almost everything I did. I played on golf courses where I had won and I came into the tournament playing well. But I put more pressure on myself because the U.S. Open does come around just once a year. It became bigger than life to me. I finished second once and third and fourth, and was even leading going into the last day."

PASSING A LEGEND: "Sam Snead was very kind when I broke his record. He called me. We had played together in a mixed team competition. I didn't try to win tournaments for recognition. My feeling is that it's going to be in the record book anyway. When I'm long gone and people look back, my name will be there at some point. It may not be at the top, but it will probably be in the Top 5. The wins I had were very special to me, and I feel real lucky."

TAKING DEAD AIM: "[Studying from noted instructor Harvey Penick] was a glorious thing, and one of the reasons I was as successful as I was. Not only was he a wonderful teacher. He was just a wonderful man. I don't know if any of us realize what an impact he had on us, not only through the golf but with his own demeanor, how he conducted himself. He never had an unkind word to say towards anybody. He would teach anybody if they really wanted to learn to play. I miss him every day."

Tiger Woods

April 10, 2003

Dear Dr. Cherney:

By far the most memorable shot I have hit as a professional was at Hazeltine last year in the PGA Championship.   I was unable to finish Friday's second round due to bad weather and came back early on Saturday morning to play the tough par-4 18th hole, where I pulled my drive into the left fairway bunker.   Not only did I have a poor stance and have to stand closer to the ball than I wanted, I had an uphill shot of about 200 yards with big trees in front of me.   It was a do-or-die shot and I hit it perfect, wound up 18 feet from the hole, and made the birdie putt to shoot 69.   I felt like I was looking at a bogey and somehow turned it into three.

Sincerely,

Tiger Woods

Tiger Woods

With eight professional major championships and 39 tournament victories, Tiger Woods has reserved a spot among golf's Mt. Rushmore, joining Jack Nicklaus, Ben Hogan, and Bobby Jones. Woods, who has excelled at every level in the game, was the leading money winner and Player of the Year in 2003 for the fifth straight year. Woods, 28, has been ranked No. 1 in the world since 1999.

Any summary of Tiger Woods' greatest shots faces one inescapable limitation: The list is destined to be obsolete, and soon. Almost every week, Woods comes up with another gem. Here are three that deserve consideration:

1996 U.S. AMATEUR: Trying to become the first to win the event three years in a row, Woods was one down with two holes to go to Steve Scott at Pumpkin Ridge in Oregon. On the 35th green, Woods sank a 30-foot birdie putt to square the match, celebrating with his traditional fist pump. He won the match on the second extra hole.

2000 PEBBLE BEACH NATIONAL PRO-AM: Seven shots back with seven holes to go seemed an insurmountable deficit, even for Tiger Woods. But Woods pulled it off, thanks to a 97-yard eagle on the par-4, 15th hole. The ball landed a few feet away and drew back into the cup. Woods defeated Matt Gogel by two shots. With the victory, Woods became the first since Ben Hogan in 1948 to win six tour events in a row.

2000 CANADIAN OPEN: Holding a one-stroke advantage on the 72nd hole, Woods knocked his drive into a bunker. From 218 yards away, Woods hit an incredible six-iron approach over the water, the ball finishing about 18 feet behind the hole in the first cut of rough.

August 5, 2003

My best shot, or at least the most memorable, was the 30 foot putt I made on the 72nd hole of the 1973 Colgate Dinah Shore Championship at Mission Hills C.C. in Palm Desert, CA to win my 82nd and last tournament.

We were playing in 20 mile per hour winds. I was in the next to last group in front of Joyce Kazmierski. I needed par to tie or birdie to win. It was the last tournament my long time teacher, Harry Pressler saw me play. It was also the last tournment I was able to play in golf spikes. Shortly thereafter I had surgery to remove a neuroma from my left foot and had to play in sneakers from then on.

I have seen many great golf shots during my career, but one that stands out was in 1958 at the Titleholders tournament in Augusta, GA. I was paired with the great Patty Berg. On the par 3 6th hole she pulled her tee shot into a greenside bunker. Her ball was on a sever downslope with a "fried egg" lie. She put the ball within a foot of the hole and made her par. She was without a doubt the greatest trap shot player I ever saw.

Mickey Wright

Mickey Wright

Mickey Wright is golf's Greta Garbo, keeping a low profile since her playing days ended in 1980. Like Garbo, Wright was a huge star, with 82 victories (second behind Kathy Whitworth), including 13 major titles. She won the U.S. Women's Open four times in seven seasons—1958, 1959, 1961, 1964—and the Vare Trophy (lowest stroke average) five years in a row. Wright, 69, resides in Florida.

LARGER THAN LIFE: "I played with Mickey my very first event as a professional. I got on the first tee, at 19 years old, and wanted to throw up. I was so nervous. Mickey Wright was bigger than God at that point in my life. Every time I played with her, I was in awe. She had the most perfect and beautiful golf swing. When you played with her, you got so caught up in watching her. There wasn't anybody better than Mickey Wright, the way she would maneuver her way around the golf course."—*Donna Caponi*

THE STANDARD: "I've watched Annika and the other players of today, but, to me, she is still the best. Anytime they compare anybody, they should be compared to Mickey. The woman was head and shoulders above all of us. She was a great role model. She was terribly high-principled. Many times, I went to Mickey for advice. I knew she wouldn't pull any punches."—*Kathy Whitworth*

NO MATCH: "She drove the ball high and a long way, and could hit a long iron high and drop it soft when equipment didn't necessarily aid you in any form or fashion. Trying to beat her was like trying to beat nobody else. There was just something about the way she played the game that was different."—*Judy Rankin*

Your Greatest Shot

_____

_____

_____

_____

_____

_____

_____

_____

_____

_____

_____

_____

My Greatest Shot

Growing up in Toronto, Canada in the 50's was a kid's delight. Hockey in the winter, golf in the summer. What could be better for an eight-year old? Humber Valley was a public course close to my home where for 55 cents, you could play all day. There were about 10 kids on my block between the ages of eight and ten whose parents would drop us off at the course early in the morning and not see us again until the aurora borealis would fire up its green and yellow hues over Ontario.

The first hole was a 500-yard par 5 which for us, seemed two miles long. Forget getting home in two. It took many shots for us to get on the severely elevated green. It was a spring day with patches of snow still on the ground, when I dribbled 4 shots to the base of the hill in front of the green, I had about 40 yards to go. My Gene Sarazen Wilson starter set had a 3,5,7, and 9-iron. The 9 iron was the club of choice. I caught it clean and managed to get it airborne, which was a feat in itself. It disappeared over the crest of the hill onto the green. I scrambled up the slope to see what I had left. A thin 30-foot line in the early morning dew curving from right to left straight into the hole told the story. My first par!!!

I immediately took the ball out of play and slept with it for about two weeks until my cocker spaniel Corky buried it somewhere in our backyard. I would hit better shots or more important ones later in life but none that opened my eyes to the joy of the game as much as that one did. I was hooked. Golf was going to be a big part of my life from that moment on.

The Greatest Shot I Ever Saw

Having watched the game of golf since the late 50's, I have probably seen most of the great shots that have made modern golf history. Watson's chip-in at Pebble to clinch the 1982 US Open, Jerry Pate's 5-iron to the 18th green to insure his Open win, Nicklaus's one iron to the 17th at Pebble that hit the stick, Couples' shot on the 12th at the Masters that hung on the bank instead of sucking back into the water, or Pavin's 4-wood to the 18th at Shinnecock for his first major.

The shot I saw did not have any historical or dramatic relevance but was most incredible. Vijay Singh was playing in a made-for-television outing with 8 other pros when they decided to try and hit left-handed shots over a lake on a par 3. The yardage was about 160. I'm not sure if Singh borrowed a left-handed club or turned an 8-iron around, but he hit a high, floating shot to about 6 inches from the hole. The other pros howled in amazement.

MICHAEL ARKUSH

I think about it every time I drive down Washington Street in La Quinta, near Palm Springs. I see the sign, "Rancho La Quinta Country Club," and flash back to the afternoon of January 19, 1999.

I didn't come to play. I came to work, to interview actor William Devane for an article on celebrity golfers. I was very excited. I had heard so much about Devane, who grew up a few houses away from me in Albany, New York. He was a hero on Bancker Street, our small universe, when he portrayed President Kennedy in *"The Missiles of October."*

I met him on the driving range. After a few minutes, Devane asked me if I had my clubs. *Did I have my clubs?* Someone had failed to show up for the charity event. Besides Devane, our group would include PGA Tour veteran Robert Gamez, and another amateur. I imagined it would be a memorable day. It sure was.

We arrived at the par-3 4th hole. With a little breeze, the hole was playing, I believe, about 180 yards. I choked up on a 3-wood. I hit it cleanly, though the ball seemed headed for a slope left of the green. Fortunately, it landed at the perfect angle, veering sharply to the right. I might even have a decent putt at a birdie, I figured.

To this day, the next few seconds remain fuzzy no matter how much I wrack my brain for the precise details. All I know for sure is that the ball kept rolling and rolling and rolling...and then disappeared. Soon, Devane, Gamez, and a few others were circling me as if I had just won The Masters.

I couldn't talk. It's funny, but I always thought that if I ever did get an ace, I'd jump up and down. I'd hug every stranger in sight. Instead, I was in total shock. I was somewhere else, somewhere I had never been. That feeling pretty much went on for the rest of the day, and for the day after that.

That is not the end of the story. For my ace, I won a golf cart. I couldn't, of course, take the cart back to Connecticut. So I sold it, using the money for my wife and me to go to Venice. I turned the cart into a gondola.

Speaking of Italy, I try to catch up with Devane at his Italian restaurant every time I visit the Palm Springs area.

[signature]

Michael Arkush

— Captions —

— Acknowledgments —

irst and foremost, we are extremely grateful to all the players who shared their wonderful stories and agreed to be interviewed for this book. We regret there was not enough space for every contribution. They are not merely accomplished golfers: They are class individuals. No wonder they have been so successful in the pursuit of their beloved profession.

We also want to thank the agents and managers and others in the golf industry who made our job so much easier. They include: Mitch Albom, Jeff Austin, Arellea Bowers, Howard Bowers, Corey Britt, Jay Burton, Kim Callazzo, Gida Campbell, Tina Carleton, Bob Combs, Marlene Crampton, Sharon Elder, Kelly Fray, Mark Freeland, Adam Freifeld, Al Fuente, Jan Gayler, Linda Giaciolli, Doc Giffin, Howdy Giles, Vinny Giles, Michael Hantman, Alissa Herron, Bill Homeyer, Astrid Jacklin, Alastair Johnston, Clarke Jones, Kimberly Julian, Rima Katorji, Rich Katz, Robert Kraut, Nonie Lann, James Lehman, Alan Levine, Tommy Limbaugh, Pat Marshall, Julius Mason, Jill Maxwell, Eric McClenaghan, James McCumber, Beverly Mikesell, Patty Moran, Beth Murrison, Laura Neal, Rick Nichols, Bev Norwood, Marlo Pronovost, T.R. Reinman, C.J. Roberts, Carlos Rodriguez, Joel Schuchmann, Ann D. Snead, Alana Snyder, Mark Steinberg, Brian Stevens, Barry Terjesen, Richard Thompson, Colleen Toledo, Scott Tolley, Dana von Louda, Kathy Widick, Connie Wilson, and Sharon Yates.

There are also our numerous friends and family members who put up with endless stories, displaying a level of tolerance well beyond the call of duty: Richard Ackerman, Charlene Alfonso, Noel Anenberg, Jeff Balton, John Baltzersen, Lorenzo Benet, Fred Bernstein, Tasha Browner, Tim Caldwell, Benji Cherney, Carrie Cherney, Claire Cherney, Nat Cherney, Gene Cofsky, Shelly Coleman, Diana Contreras, Rick Corleto, Tom Cunneff, Paul Duarte, Jerry Einziger, Allen Entin, Brent Fieland, Rory Fields, Neil Freedman, Roger Friedman, Dennis Forst, Ben Goldman, Jan Goren, Greg Hack, Bruce Kanter, Rick Katz, Mike Kesner, Ted Kruger, Gary Lazar, Leon Lewitt, Gordon Mace, Elliot Mahn, Alan Mandelberg, Doug Meadows, Eric Meyer, Megan Meyer, Richard Nussbaum, Joshua Peck, Diane Perez, Edward Price, Andy Ratner, Marty Refkin, Mike Rudman, Paul Schaeffer, Donna Schienle, Harley Schrager, Brad Shames, Andy Shapiro, Jade Shipman, Sy Silverstein, Bruce Smiley, Joel Steiger, Rob Stone, Mark Taylor, Keith Thykeson, Jack Tiano, Lisa Vitale, Celia Wiseman, Barry West, and Loyd Wright.

We owe a tremendous amount to our agent, Jay Mandel, and our editor, Matthew Benjamin.